DAY OF DEVASTATION

Photos & Stories of Alabama's Deadliest Tornado Outbreak

The Birmingham News   The Huntsville Times   PRESS·REGISTER

The Birmingham News Multimedia
2201 Fourth Ave. North
Birmingham, Alabama 35203
205-325-2237

Graphic design by Teresa Brooks, Brooks Creative Media
Cover design by Adrian Gonzalez

ISBN 978-1-57571-026-6

Library of Congress Catalog Control Number: 2011907610

Printed in the United States of America

This book is available individually or in quantity at special rates for
your group or organization. For further information, contact:
The Birmingham News Multimedia
2201 Fourth Avenue North
Birmingham, Alabama 35203
205-325-2237

Table of Contents

8   Introduction

10   The Beginning

15   First Wave

23   Marion, Franklin and Lawrence Counties

35   Limestone and Madison Counties

45   Tuscaloosa County

65   Jefferson County

82   St. Clair and Calhoun Counties

87   Walker County

93   Cullman and Marshall Counties

104 DeKalb and Jackson Counties

111 Hale and Bibb Counties

114 Elmore and Tallapoosa Counties

117 Hope Rising from Tragedy

120 Storm by Storm

127 Fatalities

Gov. Robert Bentley is shown visiting Birmingham on April 29, 2011, to see the damage from the tornado. He first visited Children's Hospital and then went to tour Pratt City. Gov. Robert Bentley (white shirt, center) talks with Mayor William Bell (at left) and Art Faulkner (at right), the Govenor's Emergency Management Director, on the tour of Pratt City.

ROBERT BENTLEY
GOVERNOR

STATE OF ALABAMA

Dear Reader:

On April 27, 2011, our state witnessed a natural disaster of historic proportion as more than 50 tornadoes devastated the State of Alabama.

Our state has never experienced a natural disaster of this magnitude. The loss of life and property has been enormous. To those Alabamians who lost loved ones, homes and livelihoods, we grieve with them and pray for them as they go through this difficult time.

I have never been more proud to be an Alabamian. Since this tragedy, we have seen the true character of our state. Alabamians care about one another. We take care of each other. Volunteers from every corner of the state have offered hope and support to their fellow citizens in a time of almost unendurable adversity and helped make it bearable.

As we slowly emerge from the tragedy, there is a spirit in this state unlike any I've seen before. The people of Alabama are strong and courageous – and our ability to do great things has no limits.

Although we will never forget the suffering and tremendous loss of the people of this state, we will see that this state is rebuilt. It is a daunting task, but I have no doubt that we are up to it.

The road to recovery will be long and hard. But I will share that road with you, as it leads to a greater, stronger Alabama.

Sincerely,

Robert Bentley
Governor

Preface

April 27, 2011 is a day Alabama will never forget.

It was the worst natural disaster in our history, a day when more than 50 tornadoes hit Alabama taking the precious lives of more than 230 Alabamians. Our hearts and prayers go out to all those families grieving the loss of loved ones.

The overwhelming response in the aftermath of the storms showed the true character of Alabamians. The quick response was commendable: First responders, voluntary firemen, the Alabama National Guard, emergency management teams, hospitals, churches and other faith-based organizations, charities, utility workers, corporations and caring citizens all deserve recognition and praise.

The true spirit, and the overwhelming resilience of our state, comes from the people. We've shared countless stories of people helping people — senior citizens, parents, college students and school children working side by side in churches, shelters and in the heart of the communities that took a direct hit. The spirit of unity is one we must not allow to wane. We must remain committed to each other.

In this book, Day of Devastation, journalists from The Birmingham News, The Huntsville Times, Press-Register and our Tuscaloosa Bureau share stories of tragedy, loss, courage and faith through pictures and words. Nothing can change what happened on that day, but we can remember those who lost loved ones through the stories told by the pictures. Collectively, our newsrooms have more than 300 people dedicated to telling the stories that affect our lives, our families and our communities. We intend to keep the spotlight on the long and challenging recovery, and have a team of dedicated reporters and editorial writers to keep you abreast of the progress.

Our three newspapers make up Advance Alabama, and we are proud to be a part of the Newhouse organization. And, we were proud to donate $1 million to American Red Cross Alabama recovery efforts through the Samuel I. Newhouse Foundation. In addition, we are donating a portion of the proceeds from every book sold to the Governor's Emergency Relief Fund.

In the words of Governor Bentley, "We cannot — and we will not — let these people down. As leaders of this state, we will see that Alabama is rebuilt."

Bob Ludwig, Pam Siddall and Ricky Mathews

Bob Ludwig is president and publisher of The Huntsville Times, Pam Siddall is president and publisher of The Birmingham News and Ricky Mathews is the president and publisher of the Press-Register and president of Advance Alabama.

The Huntsville Times   The Birmingham News   PRESS-REGISTER

Acknowledgements

Many staff members of The Huntsville Times, The Birmingham News and Mobile Press-Register worked countless hours to tell the story of the April 27 storm tragedy both for the individual newspapers and for this book.

Bob Carlton, Birmingham News senior writer, did a masterful job of taking stories from many other writers and assembling them in a format suitable for book publication.

At the same time, Walt Stricklin manned the central gathering point for photographs from The News, The Times and the Press-Register.

News librarian Amber Long gathered stories from the electronic files and organized them in folders.

At each newspaper, staff members fed in their information.

Contributions from The Huntsville Times came from writers Keith Clines, Paul Gattis, Mike Marshall, Pat Ammons, Crystal Bonvillian and Challen Stephens. Photos came from Robin Conn, Dave Dieter, Glen Gaeske, Bob Gathany, Michael Mercier, John Perry and Eric Schultz,

From The Birmingham News, contributors include writers John Archibald, Joseph Bryant, Victoria L. Coman, Charles Dean, Anita Debro, Kent Faulk, Greg Garrison, Charles Goldberg, Jeremy Gray, Don Kausler Jr., Veronica Kennedy, Dawn Kent, Marie Leech, Mike Oliver, Lisa Osburn, Greg Richter, Carol Robinson, Anne Ruisi, Jeff Sentell,

William C. Singleton III, Thomas Spencer, Chanda Temple, William Thornton and Michael Tomberlin. Photos came from Mark Almond, Michelle Campbell, Tamika Moore, Jeff Roberts, Joe Songer, Linda Stelter, Beverly Taylor, Bernard Troncale, Hal Yeager and Frank Couch.

From the Mobile Press-Register, Izzy Gould supplied both stories and photographs.

Members of The News' copy desk edited the content while still performing their regular daily tasks. They include Nichelle Hoskins, Joe Crowe, Nikki Seaborn, Greg Richter, Patrick Hickerson and copy desk chief Brian Crowson.

Graphic designer Adrian Gonzalez created the cover.

As Alabama continues the long process of clean-up and recovery in the months following April's tornado outbreak, more stories, photos and video are available at al.com, the online home of The Birmingham News, The Huntsville Times and The Press-Register: http://www.al.com/weather/april-27-2011-tornadoes/

Introduction

by Chris Darden
Meteorologist in charge of the
Huntsville National Weather
Service office

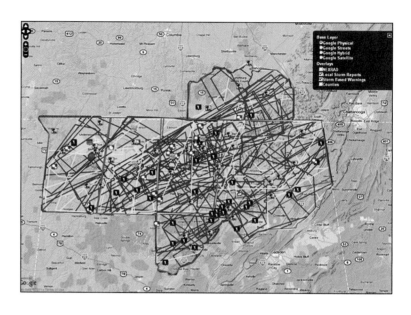

On April 27, an unprecedented natural disaster unfolded before our eyes as dozens of tornadoes raked the state. Many were violent, long-track tornadoes.

Not since 1925 has the loss of life been so great in a single day by tornadoes in the United States. In a blink of an eye, well-constructed homes were turned to rubble, trees were stripped of their bark, and churches and businesses were taken to the ground.

The National Weather Service has a mandate to protect "life and property," and we have worked diligently to do so for more than a century. Technology has increased greatly in recent decades with Doppler radar technology allowing forecasters to view the wind flow and rotation within storms, high resolution satellite imagery that shows fronts and other features critical to tornado development, and computer models that better predict the evolution of weather in the upcoming days.

In the days preceding what is now referred to as the Super Outbreak, meteorologists became increasingly concerned about this being the "big one." Sadly, even the dire predictions were well below reality. This event will go down as the most tragic tornado outbreak in modern times and will likely be the benchmark upon which all future research is constructed.

To prepare, the NWS office in Huntsville started briefing emergency managers, first responders and local media more than 48 hours in advance that this would be a major outbreak. We knew it was coming. When I woke up at 4 o'clock on Wednesday morning, I looked at the radar on my phone to see storms approaching from the South and West and knew that it was potentially even worse than I could have imagined. If tornadoes were on the ground at 4 a.m., what would the rest of the day hold? By the time I arrived at work around 5, the initial damage reports were rolling in. No matter how long you've done this job, or how many times you've been in this position, nothing prepares you for some of the calls you have to take or some of the things you see.

As the first wave rolled through and the next wave began to move in from Mississippi during the mid-morning, it was obvious there would be no breaks for the area that day. Some locations were hit multiple times; the same houses damaged in the morning and wiped clean in the afternoon.

I talked to one man who was called to his home in East Limestone after the morning storms and was busy tarping his house when the sirens blew again. A few minutes later he and his wife rode out the tornado in their shower, landing on top of a neighbor's pile of rubble.

Then came the "big ones"; the final and most intense group of supercells began to organize across Mississippi and western Alabama. We all had a sinking feeling. By early- to mid-afternoon, conditions were optimal for long-track, killer tornadoes. Every storm on the radar was showing signs of rotation, but soon the situation would get even more dire. First it was the Cullman storm. Confidence was high that a tornado was occurring, and there it was on the local skycam. But to top it all off, there was the storm moving up through Hackleburg and toward Phil Campbell with winds of at least 200 mph.

Forecasters often refer to a "hook echo" as a definitive sign of a tornado. Well, this storm had something more: a well-defined debris signature where the radar was not picking up rain or hail, but was actually picking up large chunks of debris like roofs, plywood or trees. That's when you know that things are bad.

Let's be clear: We are all professionals and we all have a job to do. However, as this storm rolled through Mt. Hope and then toward Tanner, we were all visibly shaken. Damage reports were slow to roll in from a few locations, and we knew why. It wasn't because this wasn't a damaging tornado, but because there was nobody left to report the damage. In our gut, we knew that there were

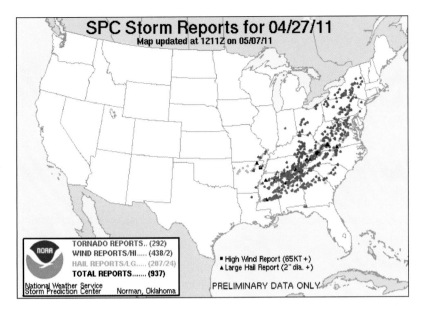

SPC Storm Reports for 04/27/11
Map updated at 1211Z on 05/07/11

TORNADO REPORTS.. (292)
WIND REPORTS/HI..... (438/2)
HAIL REPORTS/LG...... (207/24)
TOTAL REPORTS....... (937)

National Weather Service
Storm Prediction Center   Norman, Oklahoma

■ High Wind Report (65KT +)
▲ Large Hail Report (2" dia. +)

PRELIMINARY DATA ONLY

Left: Red dots streaking across Alabama, sometimes so close together that they form red blobs, show graphically how Alabama suffered from the April 27 severe weather system. The map was prepared by the National Weather Service Storm Prediction Center.

Opposite page: This National Weather Service map of the Huntsville NWS responsibility areas reveals the huge number of warnings issued during the one day of tornado outbreaks April 27. The warning areas boundary lines create what meteorologists call warning polygons. On this day polygons overlapped polygons over and over.

mass injuries and very likely a large number of fatalities. We could only pray that our warnings, updates and diligent work could prevent this from being a complete catastrophe.

In the days that followed the destruction, our staff worked many 16-plus-hour days surveying damage, providing incident support to first responders and just being there for the community. Our staff was fortunate as we had little damage as a whole, and no injuries or loss of life. As I traveled our area from Tanner to Harvest to Huntland to Higdon to Oak Grove to Phil Campbell, I gained a greater sense of pride in our community with people helping strangers, stopping to hand out food, or stopping to see if you need a ride to a shelter.

I also became frustrated by the lack of national coverage concerning the plight of our communities. Many areas were devastated just as badly as Tuscaloosa, and a few may never recover. For some reason, I feel these people deserve better and have somehow been forgotten in the 24-hour news cycle of today. The scenes of destruction out there are sobering, even for a seasoned meteorologist and someone who has been on nearly 50 storm surveys. Seeing a house with anchor bolting completely obliterated in Oak Grove was sobering. His neighbor is still looking for a Ford Crown Victoria that was

completely taken away. Seeing entire neighborhoods in northwest Madison County brought to the ground was horrendous. The scene along Rosie Road in Tanner is gut wrenching, and just walking down Brown Street in Phil Campbell is too much to bear.

The storm was so powerful there that it pulled the pavement out of the ground. Just think about the force involved there for a minute.

But that's a mere sampling of the catastrophic damage that stretches for as far as the eye can see. But the stories of survival are also uplifting. I think of the many people who praised the warning system for saving their lives,

and the many that showed us their storm shelters and where they went to ride out the storm.

We found a family of four in Higdon who somehow were left untouched in their house when everything else was swept clean around them. There wasn't even any rubble left, and their propane tank was lofted directly over their heads, missing them by a few feet.

Those are little pieces of joy and optimism in the large sea of despair. Our community will recover and we will move forward, and the NWS will continue to work tirelessly to protect our citizenry when the next threat approaches.

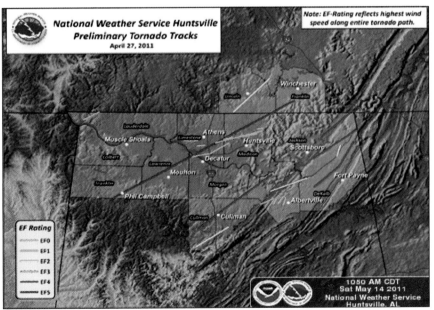

National Weather Service Huntsville
Preliminary Tornado Tracks
April 27, 2011

Note: EF-Rating reflects highest wind speed along entire tornado path.

EF Rating
EF0
EF1
EF2
EF3
EF4
EF5

1050 AM CDT
Sat May 14 2011
National Weather Service
Huntsville, AL

Huntsville meteorologists developed this preliminary route map of the severe tornadoes that struck that office's area of responsibility.

9

The Beginning

The pieces were in place for the perfect storm.

On the ground, wind blew out of the southeast at 15 to 30 miles per hour.

High in the atmosphere, at 30,000 to 40,000 feet, a crosswind came out of the southwest or west at 80 to 100 miles per hour.

The air was heavy with moisture from the Gulf of Mexico, with dew points in the high 60s and low 70s. And the day was hot for late April. Temperatures topped 84 degrees in Tuscaloosa and Birmingham.

On April 27, those conditions combined to fuel the deadliest tornado outbreak in Alabama in almost 80 years, claiming at least 238 lives, destroying thousands of homes and changing the landscape of Alabama forever.

In the Birmingham metro area, the severe weather started about 5:30 a.m., with winds as high as 100 mph doing serious damage to homes and business in Cahaba Heights and Moody.

Throughout much of the state, sunny and clear skies followed that first round of storms, but the National Weather Service and TV meteorologists warned that the worst was yet to come.

By mid-afternoon, in small towns and major cities, folks all across Alabama kept track on their TVs, radios, laptops and iPhones, as an intense cluster of storms marched through the state.

As storms drew closer to their towns and their neighborhoods, barreling down their streets and howling at their front doors, families hunkered down in their basements and bathtubs, hiding under mattresses and holding on for their lives.

And they prayed.

• • • • •

In Tuscaloosa, University of Alabama baseball players Josh Rosecrans and Nathan Kennedy heard a rumble outside their Forest Lake house and looked out to see a massive funnel cloud in the sky.

They scrambled to the bathtub, and took cover under a mattress.

Rosecrans prepared to die.

"I thought it was our time to go," he said. "We were just kind of at peace with it."

After they walked away without a scratch, though, Rosecrans pointed to a Bible verse that had been taped to their bathroom mirror.

"The Lord will guard you from all evil," it read. "He will guard your life."

• • • • •

SPC DAY 1 CATEGORICAL OUTLOOK
ISSUED: 0610Z
VALID: 27/1200Z-28/1200Z
FORECASTER: JEWELL/ROGERS
NOAA/NWS Storm Prediction Center, Norman, Oklahoma

Categorical Outlook Legend:
TSTM   SLGT   MDT   HIGH

The National Weather Service saw Alabama's bad weather coming. This national forecast outlook map was issued by the NWS Storm Prediction Center at 7 a.m. April 27, about eight hours before the supercell tornadoes rolled through the northern half of the state.

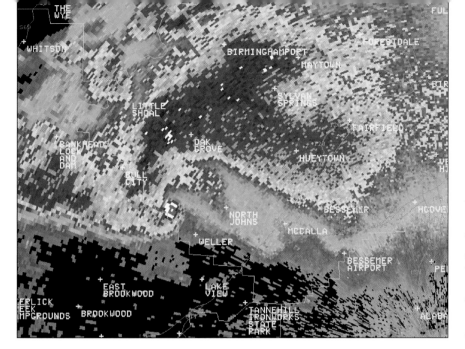

This National Weather Service radar reflectivity map shows the tell-tale hook of the Tuscaloosa/Jefferson tornado as it ripped through a rural area between Brookwood and Oak Grove. The tornado is a spot of white and purple at the tail of the orange and red hook.

On Hagler Hill in the Argo community in Walker County, 70-year-old T.J. Hagler was watching storm coverage on his television when his house started to shake and his TV tumbled off its stand.

Hagler pulled two recliners back from the wall and dove under them just as the tornado ripped off his roof.

The wall behind him fell forward but was caught by the backs of the recliners, saving his life.

"I survived," Hagler said. "God's got plans for me yet."

• • • • •

In the community of Ruth, just outside Arab in Marshall County, Phillip and Ann Hallmark and seven family members huddled in their home on Frontier Road.

As they held tightly to one another, an EF4 tornado packing a 170-mile-per-hour punch reared back its mighty fist, sweeping through a pasture and taking dead aim at their house.

Five of them died in the storm, thrown about 200 yards from the Hallmarks' home.

"They were as good a people as you will ever meet," a neighbor said. "They were just kind, good people."

• • • • •

An emotional Daryln Johnson searches for a necklace with her father's ashes at her destroyed home in the Ruth community.

Bent and jumbled sheet metal lies in a pile, damage caused by early morning winds in St. Clair County.

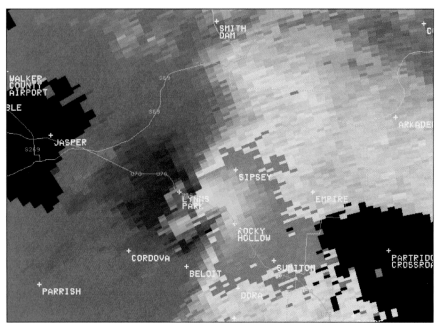

This National Weather Service radar velocity map shows the Walker County tornado as a green patch surrounded by reds and oranges, moving between Cordova and Sipsey.

In Concord, a couple of miles west of Hueytown in Jefferson County, Faye Hyde was in the living room with her three grandchildren when the sirens started going off.

Rain fell in torrents, and the sky turned black as midnight.

"We knew the weather was coming, but it happened so fast," she said.

Hyde grabbed the grandchildren, ran into a closet and fell over on top of them to protect them.

• • • • •

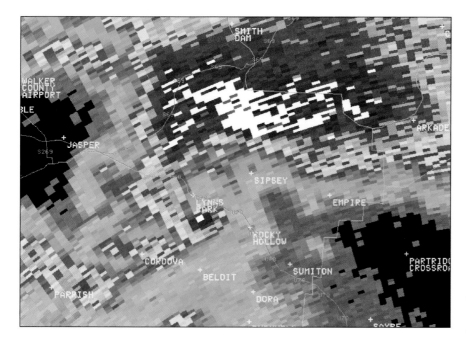

This National Weather Service radar reflectivity map shows the Walker County tornado as a right turned "hook" between Cordova and Sipsey. The orange and red hook is surrounded by greens and blues.

These few items were salvaged by Samantha Carter from her father's home in Concord, which was destroyed by the storm.

In Hale County, Sheriff Kenneth Ellis drove through pelting rain toward his 78-year-old mother's home on Hale 18 in Sawyerville.

Ellis was two miles from the house when he saw the top of the tornado.

"My cousin called me a second or two after it hit the house, just hollering for help," Ellis said.

About a mile from his mother's house, the storms had left so much debris on the road that Ellis and a deputy had to take off on foot.

They arrived to find Ellis' mother, his sister, his niece and cousin alive and safe.

The house his mother built 38 years ago was destroyed.

"We are fine," the sheriff said. "We will rebuild somehow

♦ ♦ ♦ ♦ ♦

In the town of Toney in northern Madison County, Gregory Braden, who drove a truck for the U.S. Postal Service, refused to leave his trailer at the end of Welcome Home Village Drive.

A neighbor had built an underground storm shelter, but the pump stopped working long ago and Braden didn't want to step into the foot-deep pool of stagnant water.

"The guys tried to get him to come

inside the shelter, and he wouldn't come," a friend said.

Braden told his neighbors that this was Alabama and he wasn't afraid of the tornado warnings.

After the neighbors crawled inside the underground bunker, the wheels from Braden's trailer landed on the shelter door.

Outside, a few feet away, Braden lay dead atop the rubble.

♦ ♦ ♦ ♦ ♦

In Marion County, in the small town of Hackleburg, where a killer EF5 tornado roared through at more than 200 miles per hour, 77-year-old Ruby Grissom was leaving her double-wide mobile home and headed for shelter when the storm smacked the complex housing the elementary, middle and high schools.

After the storm, her niece Tina Finder found Grissom 50 yards away from where the trailer once was.

Grissom was bleeding and had broken ribs, but she was alive.

The trailer was gone.

In the rubble, Finder found a book belonging to her 3-year-old daughter, Sadie, a book Aunt Ruby had read to the little girl.

The title: "One Windy Wednesday."

Westbound U.S. 280 traffic is at a standstill and the eastbound lanes are closed by trees blown into the roadway by strong early-morning winds.

First Wave

Hours before the historic outbreak of tornadoes on April 27, violent storms blew through much of central Alabama that morning, leaving a wake of death and destruction and sending an ominous warning of what was yet to come.

Winds of up to 110 mph toppled trees onto cars, houses and businesses in the first round of storms to hit the state.

Those early storms were just a prelude to what weather forecasters had been warning for days. Schools were shut down and many took a day off from their jobs in anticipation of the events to come.

In the Birmingham metro area, the severe weather started about 5:30 a.m., with winds as high as 100 miles per hour ripping through parts of the city, taking down trees, knocking out power and claiming three lives.

"It's so widespread," Mark Kelly, public information officer for Jefferson County EMA, said. "We've had damage reports from just about every area of the county."

In the St. Clair County town of Moody, Gayle McCrory of McCrory Road was killed early that morning when three trees crashed into the mobile home she shared with her husband, Dale, who was not injured.

One of the trees landed on the bed where she had been lying down, killing her instantly, a son, Jason McCrory, said.

"It's hard," Jean Howard, Gayle McCrory's mother-in-law, said. "I loved that little young lady.

"I never dreamed anything like that," Howard added. "It's so hard to give her up, but she is in a better place. She did not suffer. She was just gone, just like that."

Howard, who also lives on McCrory Road, said the storm sounded like an instant attack of rocks hitting her home.

"We've had damage reports from just about every area of the county."

Mark Kelly of Jefferson County EMA

Sandra Gayle McCrory was killed at 6:15 a.m. April 27 when three trees fell on her mobile home on McCrory Drive in Moody. Her son, David (right), is hugged by a friend near his parents' home where his mother was killed.

A huge white oak, estimated at more than 100 years old, was felled by early-morning winds and damaged Main Street Market in Warrior just after dawn.

"I hardly had time to get to my closet," she said. "I kept praying, 'Lord, please save my family and my friends.'"

Elsewhere in St. Clair County that morning, 27-year-old Precious Hartley was killed inside her home at Shadydale Mobile Home Park when high winds came through about 6:30 a.m.

Hartley and her two small children were in bed when the storms hit and sent a tree crashing through her mobile home. Her children weren't seriously injured.

In the Cahaba Heights area of Vestavia Hills that morning, 68-year-old Milton Edward Baker Sr. was killed when a tree limb came crashing down on him while he watched his son try to help a neighbor saw a fallen limb off a neighbor's car.

Earlier that morning, Baker had heard cries from across the street, and he and a neighbor came to the rescue of a woman and her 5-year-old twin boys, who had sought shelter under a stairwell.

After working his way through the demolished house, Baker calmed the woman and reached out his hand to pull her and her two boys to safety.

"They're superheroes, and they don't even wear costumes," one of the boys said of their rescuers.

"They're superheroes, and they don't even wear costumes."

Five-year-old Cahaba Heights boy after neighbors rescued him, his mother and his twin brother.

Hurricane-force winds

The storms sweeping through Alabama early that day snapped trees, damaged buildings and left more than 260,000 utility customers without power.

The National Weather Service said winds blew at near-hurricane force, and Jefferson County was among the hardest-hit areas.

The Jefferson County Sheriff's Office received 281 weather-related emergency calls between 5 a.m. and 8:50 p.m., sheriff's officials said.

Birmingham Fire and Rescue responded to nearly 40 emergencies in roughly the same time period.

At least two people were injured in the area around Acton and Caldwell Mill roads in the Rocky Ridge Fire Department district.

Michael Bartlett, assistant fire chief for Rocky Ridge Fire Department, said one of the people injured was a woman trapped inside her home at Shady Water Lane and Caldwell Mill Road.

Top: The fronts of businesses in this Cahaba Heights shopping district were severely damaged by early-morning high winds.

Bottom: Power lines and trees litter the streets of Cahaba Heights from strong straight-line winds and a tornado that ripped through the area at dawn.

Above: Sandra Smith walks near a tree that fell on her mobile home early Wednesday morning, just inches from crushing her.

Right: Sandra, who was asleep when the tree fell, is hugged by a neighbor on Trails End Lane in Moody.

Residents of a mobile home park on Trails End Lane in Moody check the wreckage of a mobile home overturned by violent winds early Wednesday morning, April 27.

Trees had fallen on her house and the house collapsed on top of her. It took firefighters about 20 minutes to get her out of the house. The woman was taken to a hospital for treatment.

Two trees crashed through Brenda Baker's mobile home in west Jefferson County, one landing on the bed where she had been sleeping just before waking up to the sound of the tornado warning sirens.

Another tree slammed through the other end of Baker's home in the 6000 block of Eastern Valley Road, but she and her African gray bird and four dogs were not injured, she said.

Baker said she was glad to come through the storm unharmed.

"All this other stuff can be replaced," she said.

Cahaba Heights destruction

Storms leveled trees throughout Vestavia Hills, particularly in the hard-hit Cahaba Heights area.

Fire Chief Jim St. John said police closed all roads in Cahaba Heights because of debris from the morning storms. He estimated nearly 80 percent of the roads were blocked by debris.

Several residents were trapped in their homes by falling trees that blocked doors, but St. John said public works and emergency crews were able to rescue residents. No injuries were reported from those trapped inside their homes, he added.

Mountain Brook Community Church on U.S. 280 had a large window knocked out of its sanctuary and trees punched holes in the roof Wednesday morning.

"The window by the balcony is blown out and there is glass and debris from that," pastor Tim Kallam said. "There's a tree through the roof of the fellowship hall. There's damage to the roof of the gym."

Numerous trees were down on and around the church campus, which

Numerous trees were blown down, damaging Mountain Brook Community Church and its campus during high winds in the early morning of April 27.

The morning storms destroyed the marquee at the Birmingham-Jefferson Civic Center.

Strong winds blew down trees and broke windows at Barrett School in East Lake.

Cary Baker, pastor of Grantswood Baptist Church, clears trees with his chain saw in the front yard of Stokes Skellie's home on Daniel Drive in Moody. The trees were blown down by high winds in the early morning of April 27.

fronts a section of U.S. 280 that had the eastbound lanes shut down after the storm.

"We're fortunate it was a time when there was no one in the building," Kallam said.

In St. Clair County, snapped and uprooted trees lined the roads in Moody and Odenville as workers and neighbors surveyed damage and began the cleanup from the morning storms.

Some were spared any damage while others had only minor structural damage.

Others weren't so fortunate as trees crashed down on homes and winds ripped through brick and steel.

No time to seek shelter

Along Alabama 174 in Odenville, R.A. Singleton and Patti Anderson returned to their homes after talking to neighbors across the street, where the top of a two-story brick home was peeled open and a truck pushed into the pool in the back.

Anderson, who lives in a mobile home, said the morning storm was like being in a car wash as wind and rain beat down on her home.

"I had never been as scared in my life," she said. "It was just sheets of water and stuff flying in the air. It hit so quickly that you could not seek shelter."

Across the street, a crowd gathered at Julia Cook's house after the storm knocked down three storage buildings and caused other damage.

"This was the garage," she said, pointing to the blank slab.

"We're fortunate it was a time when there was no one in the building."

Pastor Tim Kallam of Mountain Brook Community Church

An early-morning storm destroyed this huge hay barn on Kelly Creek Road in St. Clair County.

Neighbors gathered to help each other, bringing food, manpower and storage trailers.

Cook said one neighbor suffered minor injuries after being knocked into a wall.

"We're all fine," she said. "God was definitely here this morning."

That first destructive wave washed through, the sun came out and for much of central Alabama, work crews labored in bright sunshine through most of the day.

The wind was strong, but for many Alabamians, it was hard to find a storm cloud.

By mid-afternoon things began changing rapidly.

"I had never been as scared in my life. It was just sheets of water and stuff flying in the air. It hit so quickly that you could not seek shelter."

Odenville resident Patti Anderson

Trees litter this Moody area road. They were blown over by high winds in the early morning of April 27.

3:05 p.m.
Marion, Franklin, Lawrence Counties

The deadliest single tornado to sweep across this country in the last 56 years began in Marion County, a few miles from the Mississippi line, where the highway signs now bend toward the ground along U.S. 78 west of Hamilton.

Trees blew over, and Hamilton lost power. Yet for 10 miles, the massive storm largely churned above the wilderness, growing in ferocity, sucking moist afternoon air high into rotating clouds. Soon the system would spawn a tornado measuring more than a mile across.

The National Weather Service also saw evidence of satellite vortices, essentially twisters within twisters. Mesocyclone winds swirled along the outside edges, gusting toward the center.

The first population center it hit was Hackleburg, a quiet town of 1,600 in the northeast corner of Marion County. The still-standing water tower boasts of a high school baseball championship in 2007. The chief employer had been the distribution center for Wrangler jeans.

Six days after the storm, Tommy Quinn picked through his few recognizable belongings. He held a

Devastation in Hackleburg.

Above: Schools in Hackleburg, including the high school, were heavily damaged.

Left: Roofing metal hangs from one of the few trees standing in the tornado path in Hackleburg.

Below: Emergency personnel left sign after they checked this Hackleburg neighborhood for survivors.

The Wrangler Distribution Center is wiped out in Hackleburg.

Billy Ray Terrell, 77, is overwhelmed by the damage to his house in Hackleburg.

clamp for his piano and a picture his older brother painted years ago.

"I was thinking nothing is going to happen," the 21-year-old Quinn said as he stood near what had been his childhood home.

Listening to the weather report on TV, his sister-in-law packed suitcases with diapers and photo albums and urged the family to go to the storm shelter.

Quinn grabbed his wallet and car keys.

"It got dead quiet," he said. "Then we started hearing that rumble, that deafening roar."

On the Enhanced Fujita scale, a tornado ranks at the highest level of EF5 when wind speeds top 200 miles per hour. At that strength, brick homes are swept away. Concrete walls give way. Steel girders bend.

Of all the tornadoes on April 27, this storm that the National Weather

The towns of Hackleburg and Phil Campbell in Northwest Alabama were devastated by the April 27 tornado outbreak. A cold, steady rain made cleanup operations difficult Tuesday, May 3. Destruction at the Wrangler Plant in Hackleburg.

Service now calls the Hackleburg Tornado, the one that traveled 132 miles and passed north of Huntsville, was the only one rated EF5.

The storm is thought to have killed 70 of the 238 people who died in Alabama from tornadoes that day, and it remained on the ground for nearly 90 of those 132 miles.

In Hackleburg, at the beginning of that 90-mile trail of nonstop scarring, blank slabs provide the only evidence of missing homes.

A Chevy pickup sits unfolded as though made of paper, a thin tree piercing the truck lengthwise. Trees are shorn of limbs and bark. Rainwater swells in deep pits where root balls were ripped from the ground.

Everywhere are contents of exploded homes.

On the day of the storm, Quinn's brother, stationed at the shelter's only window, saw bricks fly by. Quinn's dad held fast to the shelter door. The steel reinforced roof seemed to vibrate. Quinn said it lifted six inches.

"It lasted about 15 seconds," he said. "It sounded like a low organ note."

Then came the cries for help.

Quinn noticed his father was bleeding. They all were covered in dirt. Quinn said the family realized the house was gone, except for one living room wall.

The calls emanated from a crater where moments earlier Emmanuel Baptist Church stood.

Above: Pews and debris scattered throughout Oak Grove Freewill Baptist Church.

Below: Danny Cole helps his girlfriend of 11 years, Teresa Fugate, up a slope near the underground storm shelter that saved their lives and the lives of 15 other neighbors in Phil Campbell. Their home was swept away and stood near the white truck in background.

Opposite page: Aerial of Phil Campbell.

"We can build these old houses back. If you could get your babies back, there would be no problem."

Lindon Miller, Oak Grove

> ## "I started running a little too late. I heard my car on the roof, (and) my walls were exploding outward behind me as I was running through the house."
>
> ### Gary Dobbs, Mount Hope

Quinn said he, his brother, his father and a truck driver — a man who appeared from nowhere and seemed to be bleeding from everywhere — began to tug at the toppled bricks.

They uncovered the pastor and his wife and several children in the church basement. Cinder blocks pinned her legs. His back was broken, Quinn said.

Quinn said some of the children had been saved by a cocked metal shelf. The trucker's semi had spun in the air nearby, its cargo breaking free. Unspooled steel covered the hill.

A policeman passed by on foot without stopping to dig, he said.

Quinn and his family brought the wounded from the church and hid once again in the shelter until a second, weaker tornado passed through Hackleburg. Cell phones still worked. They called family members for rescue.

Six days after the tornado passed, the main road through Hackleburg had been cut clear. There were no hordes of volunteers, no signs of the Red Cross, no operation headquarters.

A couple of military Humvees passed along the main drag. Everywhere, convoys of white utility trucks rolled along. The men in hard hats set new poles on streets where homes no longer stood, where there was nothing left to connect.

Perhaps the biggest blow to Hackleburg would be if the Wrangler distribution center doesn't reopen, business owners said.

The largest employer in town, the jeanswear distribution center employed about 150. It was destroyed.

Although most employees were evacuated, 13 remained and one died, according to a statement from VF Corp., which owns the business.

VF Corp. spokesman Craig Hodges said the company has not yet decided where, or whether, it will rebuild.

"'VF is evaluating options for distribution operations in a nearby location to allow people to get back to work as quickly as possible," Hodges said.

'People won't come back'

From Hackleburg, the storm followed the high ground west of Alabama 17, crossing the road before descending upon Phil Campbell.

A town of 1,055, Phil Campbell sits just over the line in Franklin County. Here, the storm bypassed

School buses rolled over and destroyed at Hackleburg K-6 School.

A homemade sign posted in a street in a devastated neighborhood in Phil Campbell.

Above: The Dollar General Store sign is buried in the rubble of the store in Hackleburg.

Left: Damage inside Hackleburg High School.

United Methodist Committee on Relief sets up a tent relief center outside First United Methodist Church in Phil Campbell.

the community college, left much of the school intact, and spared the old downtown and the Piggy Wiggly.

But the tornado ravaged the southern neighborhoods. Along the edge of the storm corridor, aluminum siding and car hoods wrap like tinfoil around the treetops. The tornado's path here seemed to be more than a half-mile wide.

Through the center, homes were reduced to rubble and blown into the hills. Chairs without legs. Trunks without limbs. Brick walls thrown 15 yards. Cars stamped into the earth.

Myron Herron, a 56-year-old carpenter at Browns Ferry Nuclear Plant, said his mother and father built a 3,200-square-foot bluff home with redwood fascia board. After they passed away, it came to him. On April 27, his Jeep flew through the house. He said the concrete pad rotated five inches.

One of his neighbors lost seven family members and in-laws in the same storm.

"I've got teddy bears, but I didn't have any before the storm," Herron said, surveying the remains of his home.

From his view, atop a hill, no surviving structures could be seen. He said people used to make mobile homes and work in textiles here, but no longer.

"People won't come back here," he said.

Despite his prediction, Herron had already mounted a mailbox in front of the ruins.

Sucked up the pavement

Tornadoes change the meaning of things.

Oak trees are no longer sturdy. Bricks are no longer heavy. Cars blow around like cotton. Homes are temporary. Maps are rewritten. And a church is no longer a building.

All along the storm path, worshippers gathered for their Sunday services on concrete slabs where churches once stood.

At Phil Campbell Church of God, Pastor Chris Burns said 150 came for "the service on the slab."

His wife, Nicole Burns, said they lost their home. The brick walls exploded outward as they hid in a hallway with their two children. She said two interior walls fell into each other, creating a protective lean-to.

When they emerged, their 14-year-old son found the body of his 10-year-old friend. They found a 14-year-old girl injured badly, lying in the street.

They dragged her to shelter before the second, weaker tornado followed. The girl lost her mother and stepfather, who were found a day later.

"We lost four neighbors on our

An overturned piano is all that remains from this home destroyed by the tornado when it went through Mount Hope.

A power crew truck on a ravaged street in the tornado path in Hackleburg.

street alone," Nicole Burns said.

Roy Gober with the Franklin County EMA said 26 people died across the southern edge of the county, about 20 of them in Phil Campbell.

"We had close to 800 structures that were destroyed," Gober said. "It's really odd. The house is either totally gone, or there was very little damage."

Widest, most unforgiving point

From Phil Campbell, the storm headed more east than north, veering slightly at times, narrowing in places, growing wider in others. At the little crossroads of Oak Grove, the tornado reached its widest point. The National Weather Service estimated the path to stretch more than 1.25 miles wide. It stripped the bark from pines along Franklin 81, knocking out brick walls but leaving the 40-foot-high frame ceiling of Mountain View Baptist.

Days later, in an area called East Franklin, the 115th Signal Battalion guarded destroyed homes against looters. A lone cow wandered the road.

Sammy Swinney, deacon at Oak Grove Freewill Baptist Church, walked hundreds of yards to find a piece of the church podium.

He said one man died in a chicken plant back toward Phil Campbell. Two more died in a brick home on the nearby ridge.

> ## "I can tell I'm still not right. "It's just like you are looking at everything all at one time."
>
> ### Doris Terry, Mount Moriah

Here, there was no clear corridor, but rather, devastation in all directions.

"Evidently, the center hit right here," Oak Grove resident Lindon Miller said.

Miller stepped from his pickup truck, parked in the driveway where his house used to sit. There was little debris, only a few bricks around the base. It had all been swept away.

Miller wasn't home when the tornado hit. He figures his 30-year-old grandson, Mike, and his grandson's wife, Kelly, left their small home for the seeming safety of his 10-year-old brick house. Their bodies were found more than 50 yards away in the pasture.

A Corvette parked at the home was thrown 641 feet, according to the National Weather Service survey.

"In minutes, all of it could be gone — two minutes," Miller said, peering into blank fields. "We can build these old houses back. If you could get your babies back, there would be no problem."

Tornado descends on weatherman

Having grown massive, the storm shaved the trees from the hills at the northern edge of Bankhead Forest, coming to a precipice overlooking the valley that gives way to Mount Hope.

Most trees snapped near the base. But hundreds of pines were doubled over, treetops attached but resting on the ground, trunks twisted around five and six times, until the wood turned soft and slack like taffy.

In the valley below, the carcasses of tens of thousands of chickens and the tin of the poultry houses had been bulldozed together and set aflame. Dozens more dead chickens were piled by the roadside, while thousands more wandered freely through the fields.

On the night of the storm, from his front porch, weatherman Gary Dobbs watched the storm pour over the hill, relaying information to Huntsville's WAAY-TV Channel 31.

Dobbs had offered his storm shelter

Firefighters and National Guard troops walk a tent up a road near Hackleburg High School. The tent was used as a food service area.

said he freed himself and used some wood to pry free the workers trapped in his shelter.

Dobbs has reported on storms for more than 30 years, and long ago was immortalized with bumper stickers that read: "Gary said it would be like this." He said he has been around tornadoes all his life, had seen them on the horizon. But, he said, "This was the first one headed straight at me."

The Hackleburg Tornado suddenly shrank, the path drawing to just 100 yards wide north of Mount Hope. But the ferocity never faded, and it continued to level 275 homes as it crossed in Lawrence County.

Loss, shock and new appreciation

A week after the tornado, debris pits fed the air over Lawrence County as a line of smoke signals pointed to the Tennessee River.

Toward the little community of Mount Moriah, the storm had

to the young workers at Oh Bryan's Family Steakhouse next door. All four had piled in.

"I started running a little too late," Dobbs said. "I heard my car on the roof, (and) my walls were exploding outward behind me as I was running through the house."

Dobbs said he ran into the closet at the back of his house. He awoke under a pile of debris. Despite cracked ribs, a bruised lung and a bruised kidney, he

Myron Herron looks over the remains of his parents' home after the tornado hit the Franklin County town of Phil Campbell.

Path of destruction from the Wednesday, April 27, EF5 tornado as it heads through Bankhead Forest toward Mount Hope.

whipped an old-growth white oak through the middle of Doris Terry's two-story frame home. The north wall had been sucked away.

Terry said the storm swept away a neighboring mobile home, killing Mike Dunn, who was found where the garage used to be. His wife was badly injured, she said, but the Dunn children were OK.

"I was in shock for a few days," Terry, said.

She noticed she was wearing her mother's pants, and she realized she didn't own any shoes.

"I can tell I'm still not right," she said. "It's just like you are looking at everything all at one time."

As strangers stop by her home to volunteer and help clear the yard, Terry says she feels compelled to give back.

"I wanted to help these people who were here helping me," she said.

The sensation of surviving the storm has been strangely uplifting, Terry added.

"I appreciate life more," she said. "I appreciate people. I appreciate the birds."

Then, as she stared at the tree that fell through her house, Terry wondered aloud: "What happened to the squirrels?"

Eye of the storm

As Evelyn Ashton held her grandson in her Phil Campbell home and the tornado hit, the house began to fall apart.

But the boy was still alive.

"Then a few minutes later, when the second tornado hit, the walls fell and that's when he died," Ashton said.

But there was no second tornado. What Ashton experienced most likely was a first hit from the front end of the tornado, then a moment of calm in the center, like the eye of a hurricane. Then moments later, the back of the tornado hit, and that's when the walls came down.

It is a rare phenomenon, but a strong possibility with the massive storm that devastated homes in Marion, Franklin, Lawrence and other counties in north and northwest Alabama. Greg Carbin, warning coordination meteorologist with the National Oceanic and Atmospheric Administration in Norman, Kan., said he's received reports like this before, after massive tornadoes.

"There were accounts similar in Greensburg, Kan., in 2003 — that there was a period of calm," he said. "That's one big tornado."

Like the Greensburg tornado, the one that destroyed Ashton's house and killed her 10-year-old grandson was the most powerful type — an EF5, packing winds of more than 200 mph.

Most tornadoes wouldn't have a calm center, or an eye, that could be experienced, because they are too tightly wound.

But this tornado was 1.25 miles wide at its peak, and it tracked 132 miles through five counties, according to National Weather Service assessments.

In Hackleburg, about 13 miles from Phil Campbell, Tim Bishop also said he felt the eye of the tornado. He was inside his downtown business, Hackleburg Hardware, when the tornado hit.

"I could see bricks flying, metal flying by the window, but then it calmed down and I went outside to go to my truck," Bishop said.

He wanted to go home to check on his family, but before he could get in the truck, a second round of high winds kicked up again, and Bishop said he was lucky to get back to his building.

When he finally felt safe, Bishop walked outside.

"I came out and said, 'My God, there's gonna be people dead,'" he said.

Black curtain close, funnel in the distance

The tornado, which surveyors say momentarily slowed to an EF4 or even high-end EF3 after Mount Hope, regained its full fury in the pastures toward the crossroads of Langtown.

Here, Mary Mayes died after being sucked out the front door of her flower store. Her brother-in-law was found under rubble in a ditch off the state highway the next day.

In all, 14 died in Lawrence County, according to Hillard Frost with the Lawrence County EMA.

"This one is worse than '74," Frost said. "More damage, more homes destroyed."

Jerry Yarbrough, a paramedic from Langtown, had raced unknowingly against the storm, reaching Phil Campbell to see the wounded wandering in search of ambulances.

At home in Langtown, his wife, Katie, saw the rain begin to spin, and hid in the downstairs bedroom. She watched the roof bounce up and away.

Down the street, the winds had peeled away the east wall of a nearby house and tossed a young boy into the pond. He survived.

At 4:28 p.m. that day, Katie Yarbrough crawled from the ruins and texted her husband: "The house is gone and mom is trapped."

Jerry Yarbrough's 77-year-old mother would require four staples in her head and suffer a broken foot, but she would survive. A board had punctured Katie Yarbrough's side. She said she rode in a police car, then a pickup, then an ambulance to reach Moulton Hospital.

A week later, she pointed south, where the tornado had passed within 800 yards in 1974.

"The exact same path," she said.

They put up the national flag and a sign that read, "God Blessed Us."

They plan to rebuild.

Raining blue jeans

In nearby Chalybeate, the storm started to expand again, reaching roughly a quarter-mile across near Hillsboro, where it erased Sonny's Bar-B-Que as it crossed U.S. 72.

Here, the storm dismantled TVA transmission lines, stomping steel towers into the red earth one after another as it approached Morgan County.

A week later, the old steel trellises, ranging from 80 to 150 feet high, had already been replaced with simpler towers, two-legged prongs poking straight up into the air.

At the last house in Lawrence County, a home with a Decatur mailing address, Randall Muston hid in his basement during the tornado. A trapped fisherman hid with him and several other family members.

"At 4:15 p.m., it took the house," Muston said.

The fisherman's pickup had been tossed a hundred yards into the sweet corn, a telltale sign of resurgent EF5 winds.

The concrete floor lifted several inches at one point before dropping back into place, Muston said. Two horses were blown away, but would return unhurt. One week later, his cat returned.

Ricky Kirby of Hatton in Lawrence County said he found an EKG in his yard from Smithville, Miss., which was hit by a separate EF5 about the same time as Hackleburg.

Bruce Box of Courtland said blue jeans rained from the sky at his home, 40 miles of the Wrangler distribution center.

"We got a pair, too," Kirby said.

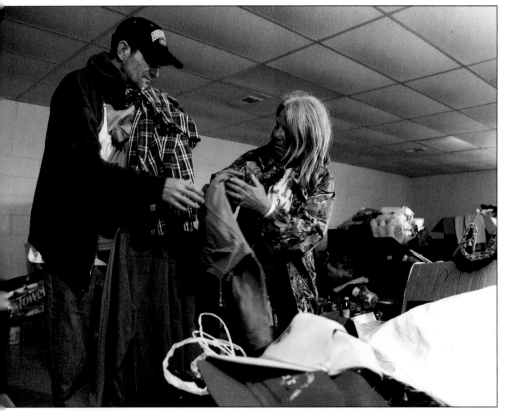

Kim Howard (right) helps Carl Tharpe find clothes in a donations center at First United Methodist Church in Phil Campbell. Tharpe lost a sister to the tornado. The church had no power and the room was lit by window light and power from a generator.

4:15 p.m.
Limestone and Madison Counties

Just before the storm hit, people in Madison County hid in linen closets, huddled in storm shelters and bathrooms, sang songs of praise and faith, and gathered under staircases.

With darkness descending in the late afternoon, with almost nothing except shades of black around them, some looked around the corner for a final glimpse before shutting the doors to their shelters or closets.

The first of the tornadoes entered Madison County just before 4:30 on the afternoon of April 27, skipping across Love Branch Road in eastern Limestone County and onto Orvil Smith Road in western Madison County, taking down trees that had been around for decades.

The exact time that the destruction began in Madison County was marked on a clock at Ford's Chapel United Methodist Church in Harvest, the oldest Methodist Church in Alabama.

It was 4:27 p.m. when the clock stopped and the tornado continued past the church and onto the Anderson Hills subdivision, site of a 1995 tornado that injured nine people and damaged 40 homes.

It was 4:27 p.m. when the power went out for days and one of the most

April Robinson, left, is hugged by her brother James Carey in front of her home that was destroyed by a tornado in Carter's Gin subdivision in Harvest.

A damaged clock from the original sanctuary of Ford's Chapel United Methodist Church stopped at the precise time the tornado hit the building.

> ## "I can't believe we don't have more fatalities."
> ### Madison County Commissioner Dale Strong

relentlessly harrowing weeks in recent Madison County history began.

"This is much worse than last time," said George Ellis, a resident of Anderson Hills whose home was damaged in the '95 tornado.

In the days that followed, most longtime county residents would agree: This was perhaps worse than any storm to ever hit this area.

"This is different, guys," Madison County Emergency Management Agency Director Rusty Russell said in the early days of the recovery.

Path of destruction

When the storm hit, it entered Limestone and Madison counties as part of the most prolific tornado track, a 132-mile swath carrying an EF5 tornado packing peak winds in excess of 200 mph.

Such a storm caused many in Madison County to call on their faith.

A preschool director in Harvest gathered her neighbors in a storm shelter under her front porch and sang "This Little Light of Mine."

A school nurse started singing "Amazing Grace" as the tornado approached. Around her, others riding out the storm picked up the final stanzas.

At Ford's Chapel Methodist Church, the steeple was blown off the roof and around a power pole on the north end of the parking lot. The church bell was hurled into a neighbor's yard.

All around the church, one subdivision after another was destroyed, leaving mounds of debris in the Carter's Gin subdivision in Toney and others.

In Anderson Hills, at the Tempo Circle residence of Eric Wilburn, there was less than five minutes to prepare for the tornado. He and his mother took shelter in a bathroom.

At the moment the storm hit, Wilburn covered his mother with his body.

"Next thing we knew, the roof was coming off and glass was breaking," he said. "In less than 20 seconds, it was over."

Farther west, on the border of

Aerial view of destroyed homes at intersection of McCauley Mill Road (on the left) and Capshaw Road.

"He died saving his family."

Maurice McGaha speaking about his brother, Ronnie

Madison and Limestone counties, large electrical transformers near the Limestone Correctional Facility were torn into shards of steel.

"I can't believe we don't have more fatalities," said Dale Strong, a Madison County commissioner, after seeing the storm damage from the air.

There were nine fatalities in Madison County. In Limestone County, there were four more.

Among them was Ronnie McGaha of Harvest, retired after 20 years in the U.S. Navy.

McGaha and his wife, Lisa, had recently remodeled their Colonial-style home on Wilbanks Lane, adding a shop where Lisa worked as a hairdresser. With the tornado approaching, McGaha, Lisa and their children, Aaron and Denae, clustered under the staircase.

Just before the tornado hit, Denae headed upstairs. Hearing the tornado roaring toward them, McGaha ran from under the stairs and toward Denae, covering her as "the house exploded," in the words of Maurice McGaha, Ronnie's brother.

The chimney fell on McGaha and his daughter. Other than bruises, Denae was not hurt. But McGaha died of internal injuries.

"He died saving his family," Maurice McGaha said.

In the Limestone County town of Tanner, a grandmother held her grandchildren tight as the storm roared onto Rosie Road.

The force of the tornado caused Roger Riddle's 18-wheeler to land on its side. His wife, Janice Peden Riddle, clutched her 4-year-old granddaughter.

"She was crazy about those kids," said Clay Montgomery, her brother-in-law.

They called her "Manny," Montgomery said.

The tornado threw her and her

National Weather Service officials walk away from a storm shelter that went unused during the storms.

husband into their backyard, far from their home, and destroyed the house.

Janice Riddle was found with her granddaughter in her arms. The granddaughter lived; Janice Riddle and her husband died.

Kenneth Montgomery, Clay's brother, was the first to see the scene.

Members of Grove Baptist clean up debris from a destroyed home in Tanner.

He pulled the grandchildren to safety, even though he had two broken vertebrae, among other injuries.

"He doesn't want to be listed as a hero," Clay Montgomery said. "He just did what he had to do."

The day after

The day after the storm hit, Madison County awoke to a sight it had seen perhaps only once before in its history: April 3, 1974.

Like the 1974 tornadoes, known as the "super outbreak," some of the worst local damage was in Tanner and Harvest.

In one way or another, though, everyone in Madison County was affected by the tornado because everyone in the county lost power.

"I don't believe North Alabama has ever been out of power at once," said Bill Pippin of Huntsville Utilities.

A dusk-to-dawn curfew was instituted. Residents were asked to get where they needed to be for the night by 8 p.m.

"We will arrest you if you are out during curfew hours and do not have a legitimate reason to be there," Huntsville Police Chief Mark Hudson said.

Electrical power and gasoline became the most precious commodities. Long lines formed immediately at gas stations. Some found gasoline in Tennessee, where they discovered more long lines.

On April 28, the morning after the storms, traffic was bumper-to-bumper on U.S. 231, the road to Fayetteville, Tenn.

Traffic was also heavy on U.S. 72,

Brother Terry Boldin delivers a message to the congregation of the destroyed Bethel Freewill Baptist Church during a service held on the church grounds.

Tornado damage in Carter's Gin subdivision in Harvest

Tornado victim Karla Newman gets a hug from neighbor John Dunham, who came by to see if he could help her. She lost her home on Mooresville Road near Athens.

Sheriff's Deputy directs traffic at the intersection of Hwy. 53 and Jeff Road in Harvest on Saturday after the Wednesday tornado.

"I don't believe North Alabama has ever been out of power at once."

Bill Pippin of Huntsville Utilities

Pam Brooks looks over what is left of her home.

the road from Huntsville to Scottsboro and Stevenson, in Jackson County.

At the Texaco station in Stevenson, the line stretched for about 200 yards, maybe 300. By noon on April 28, the station was out of gas.

With a gasoline truck scheduled to arrive from Chattanooga at around 3 p.m., some waited for three hours to fill their tanks. There were cars with tags from Madison County, Morgan County, Cullman County and Walker County.

"They're going to end up with people fighting," said Shane Brazelton of Huntsville. "They're jumping each other (in line). It's crazy."

In Huntsville, the scene was so chaotic at the Kangaroo gas station on University Drive that Lt. Col. Morris Bodrick took charge on the morning of April 29.

Only one pump on the far east end

of the station was working, and it kept going down as customers lifted pump handles on the other end of the station, releasing the pressure that was pulling the gas from the underground tanks.

With the lines growing longer and tempers shorter, Bodrick stepped up. In a booming voice, he relayed orders for Jimmy Hill, the manager of the station.

"IF ANYBODY TELLS YOU ANYTHING OTHER THAN WHAT IS COMING FROM MY VOICE, DON'T DO IT," Bodrick said.

Bodrick served in the first Gulf War and in Haiti. Now, he's the product manager for the Patriot Advanced Capability-3 missile program at Redstone Arsenal.

At about 6 a.m. on April 29, he pulled into the station "on fumes," as he put it. As the lines grew, he decided to stay as long as Hill needed him.

Volunteers from Mt. Nebo Missionary Baptist Church in Lester help burn debris for a friend on Rosie Road after the April 27 tornado destroyed many homes in the area near Tanner.

Yolanda Epp walks through the roofless house where her husband and two dogs survived the tornado that hit the Tremont subdivision off Capshaw Road in the East Limestone/Capshaw area.

"People just want instructions and guidance," he said.

One customer approached him, wondering why the police had not come to the station to keep order.

"We have to be able to self-govern ourselves," he replied. "If we can't do that, we're in trouble."

The third day

Two days after the storm, an inspiring scene unfolded in Monrovia and Harvest.

About 3,000 volunteers came to help with the cleanup. Gov. Robert Bentley was among the officials who toured the area.

"To see you here made our day,"

Volunteer workers help clear debris in the Harvest area off Lockhart Road.

Shauntaya Mitchell searches for clothing in the remains of her home that was destroyed by a tornado in Carter's Gin subdivision in Harvest.

Eddie Cosby shows the hole he crawled into as the tornado destroyed his home on Beulah Bay Road in Beulah Land.

Rodney Lucio, with the County Sheriff's Department, searches a suspected looter on Old Eli Road in the Carter's Gin community. He was detained by police.

40

said Mark Ray, one of the volunteers. "Where you go, it's a morale builder."

There were so many volunteers that volunteers at the Monrovia Community Center began asking people to park at Phillips Park, the area's youth-league baseball facility next to the center.

The majority of volunteers were expected to be in the Monrovia and Harvest area until their jobs were completed.

"There's been no talk of quitting any time soon," said Laura Strong, a coordinator for the clean-up efforts.

Strong said many volunteers arrived before 8 a.m. and stayed until dark.

"There's just a desire to help, people wanting to dig in and do something," she said.

Said one volunteer, Angelo Contino of Huntsville, "It's just what I do. Not much more to say. It's just showing them Jesus in the flesh."

A crane lifts portions of a transmission tower near Limestone Correctional Facility.

Prisoners from Limestone Correctional Facility pick up storm debris in a field as TVA workers rebuild transmission towers in the background.

Juanez Tanner hugs her grandson Jerry Tanner next to her neighbor's home that was damaged by tornados off Beaver Dam Road in Harvest.

A family sifts through their belongings in Monrovia.

Left: Volunteers ride in pick-ups while the Madison County Sheriff's Department distributes water and ice to the people on Hammond Road in Monrovia.

Above: Tornado damage of homes on Old Eli Road in Harvest's Carter's Gin community.

Left: Madison County workers clear debris from Clutts Road in the Harvest area.

View of the remains and front porch of a mobile home at 345 Yarbrough Road.

Day four

Three days after the storm, Sunday. There was more spiritual talk all around.

At Ford's Chapel United Methodist Church, Dorothy Ann Webster and others told their tornado stories.

She called them stories of faith, stories of God's word. They were stories she wanted her congregation to remember in the coming days.

"It has been an amazing week, hasn't it?" she said. "There have been some amazing experiences, and oh my goodness, the stories."

She talked of neighbors helping neighbors and friends helping friends. She talked of people reaching out to strangers, the terror of the tornadoes, the grace of survival and the pain of loss.

"I expect we'll tell these stories for a good time to come," she said. "That is good. Stories help us understand the life we live. They help us heal and grow — all important things in this time.

"They help us remember the greater story: God's story that lays over all stories."

$100,000 worth of custom motorcycles lie on the slab of a home in the Tremont subdivision off Capshaw Road in the East Limestone/Capshaw area.

Becky Smith, a volunteer with IKON/Ricoh, helps clear debris from the Carter's Gin community.

Elaine Graham, right, helps her sister Charzell Myles in Carter's Gin subdivision in Harvest.

Aerial view of the Carter's Gin subdivision in Harvest.

Ford's Chapel steeple wrapped around a power pole.

The Crenshaw family, including, from left, Tyler, Christy and David, pray during Communion at Ford's Chapel United Methodist Church. The Crenshaws' home was destroyed in the tornado.

John VanTiem, a chaplain with Hope Force, prays with Josephine Neal, whose brother Jerry Coffin's house was destroyed by the tornado in the Carter's Gin community.

4:43 p.m.
Tuscaloosa County

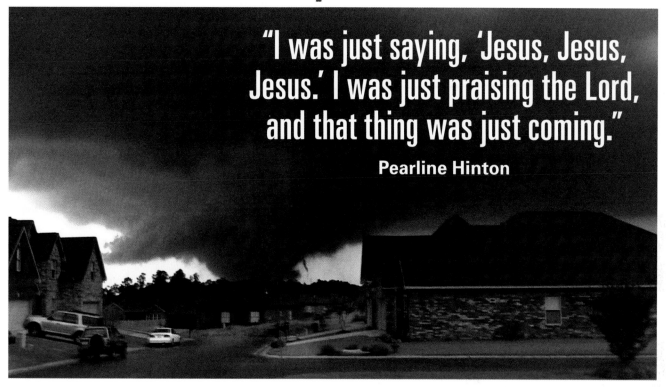

"I was just saying, 'Jesus, Jesus, Jesus.' I was just praising the Lord, and that thing was just coming."

Pearline Hinton

The leaden tornado funnel bears down on a Tuscaloosa subdivision. Photo taken looking north from Taylorsville.

Pearline Hinton and her teenage son, Kendrell, huddled together in the bathroom as a killer tornado bore down on their Tuscaloosa apartment complex.

Hinton crouched in the bathtub, and her son wrapped his arms around the toilet and held on tight.

Then he started to say his prayers.

"I was just saying, 'Jesus, Jesus, Jesus,'" Kendrell Hinton recalled later. "I was just praising the Lord, and that thing was just coming."

Not long after the tornado passed through, Pearline Hinton stood in the street in front of what remained of her apartment. Minor cuts covered her bare feet, and her hair was cluttered with tiny pieces of insulation.

A firefighter came up to her and asked if she was familiar enough with the neighborhood to help him match names with homes. Then he went to find shoes for her, retrieving a cowboy boot and another shoe that was not hers. It brought a smile to Hinton's face.

The tornado had ripped the roof off of Hinton's apartment, providing a clear view to the sky.

"I had been watching the news and I seen it coming," she said. "And I told my son to, 'Come on, let's get in the bathroom.' We got in there and everything just started crashing and breaking. Chairs and everything were flying. I mean, TVs and cars and everything."

As afternoon turned to night, reality

hit Hinton.

Where would she go? What would she do?

"I'm trying to call my siblings," she said. "Ain't nobody picking up. I ain't got nowhere to go."

Picking up the pieces

The next day, the streets of Tuscaloosa, so often congested with college students and football fans, instead looked like something out of a big-budget Hollywood disaster movie.

Homes and businesses leveled to concrete slabs.

Cars, vans and 18-wheelers picked up, tossed around and flipped upside down.

Trees uprooted and light poles bent like plastic straws.

Aerial shot reveals the devastation of a Tuscaloosa housing complex.

"We have neighborhoods that have basically been removed from the map."

Tuscaloosa Mayor Walt Maddox

Top: An east Tuscaloosa neighborhood ravaged by the tornado.
Bottom: Scattered boats, smashed boathouses and skewed piers are all that remain of a marina northeast of Tuscaloosa.

Rescue workers tend an injured 6-year-old who was pulled from rubble on Tuscaloosa's Greensboro Avenue.

Pile after pile of twisted metal, splintered wood and shattered memories.

Block after devastated block.

Late in the afternoon on Wednesday, April 27, a date that will be forever etched in this state's collective memory, an EF4 tornado ripped through Alabama's fifth largest city and carved a half-mile-wide swath of destruction that permanently changed the landscape.

"We have utter destruction," Tuscaloosa Mayor Walt Maddox said after he flew over the damage the next morning.

"We have neighborhoods that have basically been removed from the map."

The tornado claimed 41 lives in Tuscaloosa County.

On the Thursday morning after the storm, the community was still in shock as University of Alabama students and Tuscaloosa residents roamed the streets and canvassed the neighborhoods looking for family and friends, and collecting what was left of their belongings.

At the junction of McFarland Boulevard and 15th Street, a major intersection that was hit particularly hard, Danny and Vivian Lucas of Sylacauga waited anxiously to reconnect with their daughter, UA senior Krystal Stroud.

They couldn't remember exactly how to find the rental home she shared with her three roommates because all of the nearby landmarks — Krispy Kreme Doughnuts, Full Moon Bar-B-Q and the Chevron station — had been destroyed.

"I haven't got a clue where to go look for that girl," Danny Lucas said. "The Krispy Kreme Doughnuts place is one we used for a landmark, and it's not there.

"We know she's alive," he added. "We just don't know where she's at."

Just east of McFarland, on 13th Street East, where Robert and Doris Inghram have lived for about 50 years, 82-year-old Robert Inghram covered a shattered window with a piece of particle board while his wife picked up silverware that had been scattered on the kitchen floor.

A framed newspaper clipping of their son-in-law, former Alabama football star and Mississippi State coach Sylvester Croom, hung on the wall unharmed.

While the tornado tore off the front of their house, the Inghrams

A Tuscaloosa church lost its roof and one corner of the building while a business next door was flattened.

Scene is Rosedale Courts, 10th and Greensboro Avenues, Tuscaloosa, shortly after tornado struck.

weathered the storm in a bathroom in the back.

"I'm so used to trains because we live by the track," Doris Inghram said. "I was thinking it was a train, like the idiot. I just wasn't thinking."

Lives turned upside down

At a press conference the day after the storm, Alabama Gov. Robert Bentley, who has lived and worked in Tuscaloosa much of his life, said he was struck by the extent of devastation.

"It's so hard for me, being from Tuscaloosa and loving Tuscaloosa like I do," Bentley said. "It makes it even more difficult being the governor and seeing the destruction that we have here, seeing the loss of lives that we've had and just seeing how people's lives have been just turned upside-down."

Destruction from the tornado also crippled Tuscaloosa's response and clean-up efforts.

The city suffered "major infrastructure issues," Maddox, the mayor, said, noting the loss of its Emergency Management Agency headquarters, which had to be relocated to Bryant-Denny Stadium.

Most of the city's fleet of garbage and recycling trucks were either damaged or destroyed, complicating cleanup efforts and affecting garbage and recycling pickup "for the months to come," Maddox added.

One of the city's fire stations was destroyed, and two major water tanks were out of water, creating shortages, the mayor said.

While the University of Alabama campus avoided the storm's fury without significant damage, at least five students who were living off campus were killed in the storm.

One of those was Ashley Harrison, the girlfriend of Crimson Tide football player Carson Tinker.

They were with each other at Tinker's house not far from the campus when the tornado came through, picking them up and throwing them from the house.

Harrison, a 22-year-old senior from the Dallas area, was believed to have died instantly, and Tinker suffered a concussion.

"She was an amazing individual," former Crimson Tide tight end Colin Peek, a close friend of Harrison, said.

A makeshift memorial to tornado victim Ashley Therese Perret Harrison was erected amid wreckage from the storm.

Verse of Hope

TUSCALOOSA — The Bible verse was taped to the mirror in the bathroom of the house that no longer stands at 308 17th Street East. Scribbled on a notecard, it was put there by the mother of a former tenant, ex-Alabama outfielder Kent Matthes.

On the afternoon of April 27, in that bathroom, Alabama catcher/pitcher Josh Rosecrans prepared to die. He and Nathan Kennedy, a right-handed pitcher and roommate, had observed an unsettling calm outside their house in the Forest Lake neighborhood. When they heard a rumble and then saw a power flash as a massive funnel cloud appeared, they scrambled to the bathtub and huddled under a mattress.

"I was just telling Nate, 'Hey, man, there went the roof,'" Rosecrans said. "For about 30 seconds, it was chaos. Everything was flying around. It was really unexplainable.

"I really thought it was just my time, I thought it was our time to go. We were just kind of at peace with it."

They walked away without a scratch.

"It was like there was a shield over our bathtub, to be honest, because that's all that was left," Rosecrans said.

But he noticed one detail in the rubble: Psalm 121:7.

"The Lord will guard you from all evil; He will guard your life."

"That thing was still taped on the mirror," Rosecrans said.

Trees along a Tuscaloosa street are stripped bare of leaves and limbs and are wrapped in metal by the storm

Rick's Hardware in Tuscaloosa, its roof collapsed and half the front torn away, sits amid a cluster of neighbor businesses, some that suffered equally and many that suffered much worse.

"She was truly gorgeous inside and out. She was a woman to be admired and who inspired other people."

As UA students came to grips with the deaths of their classmates and the destruction of their neighborhoods, the university called off classes for the rest of the spring semester and canceled final exams. Graduation exercises were postponed until August.

Sorting through the rubble

In the Forest Lake subdivision off 15th Street, the tornado toppled pine trees and ripped open houses.

Ken Shackleford, a former lineman for the Georgia Bulldogs, and his girlfriend, LaTasha Temple, a UA graduate student and athletic trainer, rummaged though the debris piled outside their rental home in hopes of salvaging photographs and other mementos.

The day before, Shackleford and Temple, who is expecting a baby in September, had taken cover under a mattress and held on for their lives.

"It was like a slow, deep rumbling," Shackleford recalled. "We thought it was just thunder, but it ended up being a lot worse.

"When I really realized it wasn't thunder anymore (was when) it lasted for, like, 15 seconds. Thunder never lasts that long. Our ears popped. I grabbed the mattress on top of us. We had our two puppies with us. Luckily, we made it through."

The morning after, as Temple sorted through the rubble, she found a box and opened it to discover a pair of ceramic cups she had purchased in Taiwan, where she had studied abroad.

She smiled at her discovery, but her boyfriend said they already have what really matters.

"We understand that all of that material stuff is nothing," Shackleford said. "We have each other, and our baby is OK."

A visit from Obama

Two days after the storm, President Barack Obama and first lady Michelle Obama came to Tuscaloosa to assess the damage and offer the government's help in rebuilding the city and others across Alabama.

As he and the first lady walked along some of the devastated streets in the Alberta City area, the president offered hugs and handshakes to survivors.

"We just took a tour, and I've got to say, I've never seen devastation like this," Obama said. "It is heartbreaking."

The president's motorcade proceeded to Holt Elementary School, which had been hard-hit by the storm and was serving as a distribution center for food, drinks and first aid.

Obama thanked Principal Debbie Crawford, who told him she and some of her teachers had been at the school for almost 48 hours helping neighbors and the parents of their students who had been affected by the storm.

"You must be tired," Obama said.

Crawford gave him weary smile and said, "Just a little, yes, sir."

Obama noted that, for all the damage and the sadness the tornados had brought to Alabama, the people he met convinced him that better days will return.

"What you're struck by is people's resilience and the way that the community has come together," he said. "And obviously, that's testimony to the leadership of the governor and the mayor, but it's also inherent as part of the American spirit.

"I've never seen devastation like this... It is just heartbreaking."

President Obama

Trees were stripped bare with the tops snapped off during the April 27 tornado in Tuscaloosa.

Football star, lucky survivor, community volunteer

TUSCALOOSA - One block from mass destruction, former Alabama football star Javier Arenas rode out the deadly Tuscaloosa tornado in his bathtub. Two days later, he rode to Kansas City, where he now is a defensive back with the NFL's Chiefs.

Then he rode back Tuesday to Tuscaloosa with his SUV filled with items to donate to storm victims. He pulled up in the University Mall parking lot Wednesday morning with a few friends, emptied his vehicle and started greeting residents who were in need.

"I want to thank the makers of my tub," said Arenas, who was alone at his house close to the intersection of 15th Street and McFarland Boulevard. He said his house is still standing, but the houses one block away were demolished.

"We had warnings the week before," Arenas said. "To be quite blunt, I didn't believe it was going to hit. I looked out my window and it was by Forest Lake. I realized it was coming straight toward where I was. It was a minute and 45 seconds of the worst sounds you could have heard.

"I was real blessed. It was a life-changing experience."

Arenas made the round trip to Kansas City with Sarah Buschmann, a triple jumper on Alabama's track team who is from Kansas City. They returned with items that were donated by members of the Alabama Alumni Association's Kansas City chapter, and they went on a shopping spree at Sam's.

Among the items Arenas was donating were animal crackers, granola bars, apple sauce, fruit cups, peanut butter, canned tuna and corn, bottled water, batteries, sun block, bug spray, toothpaste, diapers, soap, deodorant and what Arenas called "girl products."

President Obama shakes hands with Tuscaloosa residents as he tours tornado-ravaged areas of the city on April 29.

"We go through hard times, but no matter how hard we may be tested, we maintain our faith and we look to each other to make sure that we're supporting each other and helping each other.

"I'm sure that that spirit is going to continue until this city is all the way back."

Pitching in, helping out

That same day, Alabama head football coach Nick Saban, and his wife, Terry, and other UA athletic department staff members visited the Belk Activity Center to distribute Crimson Tide clothing to the tornado victims staying at the American Red Cross shelter.

The coach's visit brought smiles to many of the 700 people who were being housed at the center off McFarland Boulevard, just south of where the tornado came through. They posed for pictures and asked for autographs.

"The community spirit has been wonderful," Saban said. "I was really proud of the way the university responded — the students as well as our team.

"You can't just be a team on Saturday," he added. "You have to be a team in the worst of times. This is the worst of times for a lot of people."

As the cleanup continued throughout the weekend, volunteers Bart Wilder and Charles Anderson

navigated an ATV through the shredded remains of the Rosedale Apartments complex, the same place where Pearline Hinton had huddled in the bathroom with her son.

The vehicle's brawny wheels are made to handle unpredictable terrain, and as Wilder navigated his way through the rubble, the ground was littered with bricks and cinder blocks that used to hold together buildings.

"It looks like a bomb went off, absolutely decimated," he said. "'I've never seen anything this devastating in my life. It's shocking."

The deeper Wilder and Anderson ventured into the tornado's swath, the more somber the ride. Front steps that

Michelle Obama hugs a storm victim at the Holt Elementary School aid station in Tuscaloosa.

"You can't just be a team on Saturday. You have to be a team in the worst of times. This is the worst of times for a lot of people."

Coach Nick Saban

Alex Burch and Chase Botthof, both 6, man the "Tuscaloosa Relief Kitchen" that they and other young residents of Hoover's Preserve neighborhood set up to gather goods and raise money for Tuscaloosa tornado victims.

Uprooted trees, housing units without roofs or walls in Tuscaloosa.

Above: A police officer stands amid the rubble of Tuscaloosa's Rosedale Courts shortly after the storm passed.

Left: President Obama holds 2-year-old Isaiah Florence and rubs his hair at the Holt Elementary School aid station in Tuscaloosa.

once led to houses now led to nowhere, as homes were completely blown off their foundations, some all the way down to the dirt.

"This storm is just horrific, and it's very personal," Anderson, who graduated from the University of Alabama and was an equipment manager for the football team, said. "I just felt I had to come down here and do something."

A day of worship

That Sunday morning, Rosedale Baptist Church, which suffered major damage in the storm, held an outdoor worship service.

The tornado had peeled back the church roof and ripped off its facade. A section of the steeple was propped against a nearby fence.

But the storm's fury couldn't stop the Sunday service.

Church members and guests sat in folding metal chairs, shielded from the sun by tents normally used for football tailgating parties. The pastor, Louis Johnson, delivered his sermon from a flatbed trailer pulled behind a pickup truck.

As chainsaws buzzed in the distance and a helicopter flew overhead, about 100 church members and guests stood up to sing "Victory in Jesus."

The 32-year-old Johnson, who has been pastor at Rosedale Baptist for just a couple of months, reminded the congregation that God is good.

"As we look at the destruction around us, the first question that people are going to ask is, 'Would a good God let this happen or does God even exist?'" Johnson said. "God not only exists, but he loves us.

"Every single person here today will be here because as the damage was coming through and their homes were being ravaged and every possession they had was being destroyed.... He placed his hand over them and protected them."

Neighbors pick through the debris of what once was their homes in Tuscaloosa.

Workers search the rubble along Greensboro Avenue for survivors in the tornado's wake.

Tuscaloosa residents sift through storm rubble as the cleanup quickly begins.

Battered, scarred and jumbled cars litter the area around Rosedale Courts at 10th and Greensboro Avenues in Tuscaloosa.

Cars were overturned by storm winds at I-359 in Tuscaloosa on April 27.

Tuscaloosa, Alabama (pre-storm)

This one-meter resolution image of Tuscaloosa was collected April 4, 2006 by GeoEye's IKONOS satellite. The image was taken approximately five years before a massive tornado struck Tuscaloosa on April 27. The image was collected by the IKONOS satellite while flying 423 miles above the Earth at an average speed of 17,000 mph, or four miles per second.

GeoEye

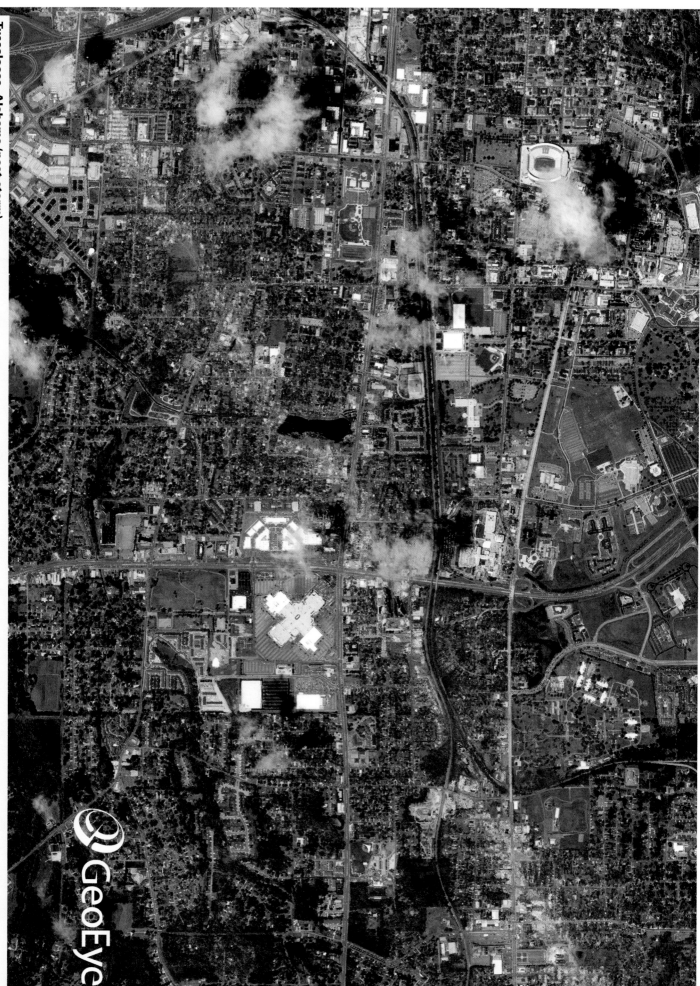

Tuscaloosa, Alabama (post-storm)

This one-meter resolution image of Tuscaloosa was collected April 28, 2011 by GeoEye's IKONOS satellite. The image shows an overview of the path of destruction (almost an eraser effect) of the devastation to Tuscaloosa after a massive tornado touched down on April 27. The "post-storm" image was collected by the IKONOS satellite at 11:35 a.m. while flying 423 miles above the Earth at an average speed of 17,000 mph, or four miles per second.

GeoEye

Western Jefferson County, Alabama (pre-storm)
This one-meter resolution image of the western part of Jefferson County, including Pleasant Grove, was collected May 13, 2001, almost 10 years before the massive tornado struck Jefferson County on April 27, 2011. The image was collected by the IKONOS satellite while flying 423 miles above the Earth at an average speed of 17,000 mph, or four miles per second.

GeoEye

Western Jefferson County, Alabama (post-storm)

This one-meter resolution image of the western part of Jefferson County, including Pleasant Grove, was collected April 28, 2011, one day after the massive tornado struck Jefferson County on April 27, 2011. The image was collected by the IKONOS satellite while flying 423 miles above the Earth at an average speed of 17,000 mph.

GeoEye

Patricia Dunn hugs her son Michael as they stand in the road that leads to his Concord home that was destroyed.

5:30 p.m.
Jefferson County

Mike Dabbs came face-to-face with a monster.

Sitting in his hilltop home in Concord in western Jefferson County, Dabbs watched on TV as a deadly tornado wreaked destruction on Tuscaloosa.

Then, when the tornado turned in his direction, Dabbs sent his wife and son-in-law into the basement with his grandchild. Dabbs and his daughter went out on his front porch to look for the tornado.

The higher elevation gave Dabbs a perfect view of the churning black funnel cloud as it chewed through the valley, taking lives and destroying homes of his friends and neighbors before heading straight for him. He and his daughter ran into the basement to join the rest of the family. The adults formed a human cocoon around the baby. "I prayed to God to protect us," Dabbs recalled. "But if He had to take somebody, take me."

All were spared.

The house was not.

Rescue workers, one carrying a litter, search for injured on a Jefferson County hillside where homes once stood.

On April 27, for Faye Hyde, the world went away.

House: gone.

Car: gone.

Life as she knew it: gone.

Barely 10 minutes after a tornado blasting 190 mph winds shredded her home in Concord, Mrs. Hyde sat on a mattress, clutching her grandchildren in the nothingness that used to be her neighborhood.

On Wednesday her world went away. On Thursday the image of Faye Hyde went into the world.

Birmingham News photographer Jeff Roberts shot a photo of Mrs. Hyde moments after she climbed from the rubble. She sat, eyes closed as if in prayer, enveloping 2-year-old granddaughter Sierra Goldsmith in a warm embrace and a wet quilt.

It was the kind of image that haunts you, that sticks with you, because it speaks at once of devastation and ruin, and of love and hope.

It appeared across the top of The Birmingham News the following day, and has appeared all over the world since, in New York and London, in a two-page spread in Time magazine. It has become a symbol of suffering and loss, of how material things seem almost immaterial in a time of so much death.

That image was everywhere. And the world wanted to know about Mrs. Hyde. Calls and questions poured in. Where was she? How was she? Are those children OK?

The 69-year-old grandmother had no idea of that interest. In her mind, she was just another person displaced by the storm, just someone else trying to hold onto family.

The Hydes have spent nights in a Bessemer motel since the storm, and days searching for memories. She and her husband, Willie, have been to Concord each day to look for family photographs.

"We found a few," she said. "Some may be salvageable."

But that's it. The house her family rented is gone; its furniture splintered and lost, and their white Ford Explorer turned upside down and dropped on a carpet store across the street.

"We'll just have to start over," she said. "Completely."

Mrs. Hyde is still shaken, but she described what happened as the tornado bore down the week before.

She and her grandchildren, Sierra and 5-year-old twins Ethan and Evan Goldsmith, were in the living room as the sirens sounded. Rain fell in waves, and the roar of the wind grew louder as the sky turned black as night.

"We knew the weather was coming, but it happened so fast," she said. "I grabbed the children into a closet and fell over on top of them. The glass started cracking, and I knew the house was gone."

Willie Hyde ran to join them but was pinned by debris. He called out but heard only wind.

"I just knew they were dead," he said. "The house just disappeared, like a magician's trick."

Mrs. Hyde covered the children while sheet rock and wood fell from above. Remarkably, they all emerged without serious injury.

The children are back in day care now, trying to return to a normal schedule. They are fine physically, but they talk of how the wind blew their house — and their toys — away.

The Hydes don't know what comes next. They're amazed by the kindness of people, but they must find a new rental home, and furnishings.

For now, they count their blessings and pick through rubble. They still hope to find a few memories, and let others go. They trust the future holds . . . something better.

Mrs. Hyde, well, she stays busy — like so many others — just finding strength to live from day to day.

And if she has become a symbol of resolve, of love amid the ruin, it's news to her. She is, after all, just trying to hold onto her family.

"I've been told the picture was in the paper," she said. "I didn't know all that other stuff."

—*John Archibald*

What once was a windbreak of stately pines is dashed to the ground along with a whole neighborhood.

'A very sad road'

Throughout western Jefferson County, the second-deadliest tornado outbreak in Alabama history cut a wide swath of death and destruction, primarily in the Concord, Pleasant Grove and Pratt City areas.

Twenty county residents died in the storms, with 10 fatalities in Pleasant Grove and six in Concord. Another 550 were injured.

About 5,700 structures, including 4,800 homes, were significantly damaged or destroyed, according to the Jefferson County Emergency Management Agency. Cleanup costs alone were estimated at $260 million, which does not include the price of rebuilding.

"It's very difficult right now for us to get our arms around what has happened to our community here and beyond our borders," Jefferson County Sheriff Mike Hale said the day after the tornado swept through the county. "The loss of life will reach a long way down a very sad road. Beyond that, the cleanup effort and restoration will be a massive undertaking.

"I keep getting asked what we need," Hale added. "Prayer right now is my only answer. We know how to search, we know how to secure. What we need is divine intervention and comfort for those that are suffering."

For many in the western part of the county, this was their second encounter with a deadly tornado in 13 years.

On April 8, 1998, an EF5 tornado roared through the area, killing 32 people and destroying more than 1,000 homes in Oak Grove, Rock Creek, Concord, Pleasant Grove, Sylvan Springs, Maytown, Edgewater, McDonald Chapel and Pratt City.

The morning after this year's storm, deputies, firefighters, police officers and the U.S. Marshal's office scoured the streets and neighborhoods of Pleasant Grove looking for bodies and survivors.

> "It's very difficult right now for us to get our arms around what has happened to our community here and beyond our borders. The loss of life will reach a long way down a very sad road."
>
> **Jefferson County Sheriff Mike Hale**

67

This swath of devastation in Jefferson County was caused by a tornado that ravaged an area from Concord to Pleasant Grove to Pratt City.

Some residents never left after the deadly twister the day before. Others found their way back Thursday morning to salvage what they could.

Some wept in the streets.

Lori McCreary stood in the rubble of what had been the home of her

Stripped trees and an overturned SUV mark the tornado's path through the Concord area.

pregnant daughter, son-in-law and grandchild. They all had found a safe place before the storm. McCreary was trying to salvage their clothes. She planned to find them a rental home to start over somewhere far away from Pleasant Grove.

"They are leaving," she said. "The community is great. The people are great. But it's just too close. It's happened here too many times."

Less than 24 hours after the tornado wreaked its devastation, Pleasant Grove police began receiving calls about looting in the area.

A few hours later, police and the U.S. Marshal's office arrested three 18-year-olds in connection with the attempted burglary of a home that had been damaged in the storm.

"We want to let the public know about these arrests," Pleasant Grove detective Jason Davis said. "We just

want to show people that we're not going to tolerate it."

If the tragedy brought out evil in a few, it brought out kindness in many others.

In the aftermath of the tornado, groups of volunteers — from church congregations to neighborhood groups — rallied to help those in Pleasant Grove.

A collective of churches — including Church of the Highlands in Irondale, Elevate Church in Hueytown, St. Luke African Methodist Episcopal Church in Birmingham and Hueytown Baptist Church — set up a station at an intersection in Pleasant Grove and handed out juice and household and hygiene products.

"We've had tremendous support," Pleasant Grove Mayor Jerry Brasseale said. "It has been unreal."

Birmingham Police officers carry an injured man along Pratt City's Dugan Avenue shortly after the storm passed. The man was placed on a gurney for treatment.

'Just total destruction'

In downtown Birmingham, Boutwell Auditorium became a refuge for those who lost everything in the tornado.

Cots lined the auditorium floor, and more than 200 survivors made it their temporary shelter the night the storm hit.

Among those were Makesha and Frederick Taylor, who had crawled into the bathtub of their second-floor apartment on Cherry Avenue when the tornado came roaring through, ripping the roof off their building. "It was the loudest sound I've ever heard when the wall caved in," Frederick Taylor recalled the next day. "Trees snapping, nails popping. It was awful.

"As far as you could see, it was just total destruction. Houses gone. Cars destroyed. People running around screaming, looking for people and couldn't find them."

Emergency workers from Pleasant Grove and surrounding communities treat storm-injured residents in the Pleasant Grove Fire Department truck bay.

Cars sit in driveways where homes no longer exist; others are blown into yards; forests are laid flat.

"Ten thousand horses came over my house and they were chasing a freight train. All I could do was scream, 'Jesus, keep us wrapped in your blood.'"

Birmingham Police Sgt. L. Roby

The Taylors made it outside and waited in the rain with others at their apartment complex until a bus came to take them to Boutwell, where they spent the night.

They returned to their apartment the next day to try to salvage their belongings.

'Had to step in'

Rick Reynolds' grandmother used to sit him on her lap and tell him stories about the tornadoes that narrowly missed her Smithfield Estates home.

On April 27, the Reynolds family wasn't so fortunate.

Of the seven houses they live in near Pratt City, five were destroyed and two were damaged.

But they were thankful no one was hurt.

"They always come through here, but we've always been lucky in the past," Reynolds said.

Built by his grandfather in 1947, Reynolds' house is surrounded by six

Above: The Sunday, May 1, Bethel Baptist Church service took place at Fair Park Arena after the Pratt City Church was destroyed in the Wednesday tornado. Overcome with emotion, Tara Bartlett and Deirdre Gaddis comfort each other in the back of the arena.

Left: Residents of Pratt City look up and down Hibernian Street, searching for missing neighbors, friends and loved ones, shortly after the storm passed on Wednesday afternoon.

others — all occupied by relatives, including his grandmother, brother and cousin.

"It's nothing but family on this street," said Rick's brother, Anthony Reynolds.

That will likely soon change. Family members said they will look for somewhere to move, rather than rebuild.

David Miller, whose house was spared, knew he had to do something to help his neighbors.

So Miller, who lives about a quarter of a mile from the devastation in Pratt City, turned his modest one-story cottage into a relief distribution center, where storm victims and volunteers came to pick up bottled water, diapers, hygiene products, children's toys, dog food and other essentials.

Miller and his friends collected items donated by the Christian Service Mission, Girl Scout troops, churches and individuals, he said.

Members of President Obama's Cabinet visited Pratt City during the week following the tornado outbreak. Birmingham Mayor William Bell walks the streets of Pratt City with Homeland Security Secretary Janet Napolitano.

Cleanup and relief continue in Pratt City, May 2, 2011, after the April 27 tornado. David Miller has set up a relief center at his house 512 Ave. Y in Pratt City. He's helped by Corey Fewell, 11, with stacking water.

"We have 15 children whose houses were completely destroyed, and others are just scared to death."

Concord Elementary School Principal David Foster

His home became a warehouse, and his front yard turned into command central.

His friends Patrina Webb and Adrienne Blackmon grilled hot dogs and hamburgers to feed neighbors who had no other means of getting a cooked meal.

Miller was motivated to act after he overheard someone say that charity groups were concerned about sending aid to his neighborhood because of reports of looting. "They said they were not going to send anything else to Pratt City," he said. "I had to step in."

'There is hope'

On the first Sunday after the storm, displaced members of Bethel Baptist Church of Pratt City hugged one another as they shared stories of loss and survival.

The 2,000-member church lost its sanctuary in the tornado and had to gather at the Fair Park Arena for its Sunday service.

Left: People walk down Magnolia Lane in Concord looking at the debris. Below: Rick Reynolds and girlfriend Kajuana Griffin clear brush from around their damaged homes. Reynolds, 53, said that his lifelong home in the Smithfield area, built by his grandfather in 1947, was heavily damaged by the tornado. That home and six others nearby were all occupied by his family. Five were left uninhabitable and a sixth was heavily damaged.

"We derive beauty from the ashes. Our faith will not refrain from the face of tragedy."

the Rev. Jesse Jackson

Their guest preacher, the Rev. Jesse Jackson, reassured them that God would provide for them.

"A new house, a new job, a new church, a new Alabama," Jackson told them. "There is hope. There is power."

Birmingham Police Sgt. L. Roby, whose Pratt City home was destroyed, hugged people as she arrived at the service.

"I'm looking for my church," she said. "I ain't got no house. I got my life. I'm all right. My children are accounted for. I've got my church." Roby had ridden out the storm in her basement.

"Ten thousand horses came over my house and they were chasing a freight train," she said. "All I could do was scream, 'Jesus, keep us wrapped in

your blood.'"

Some attending services that Sunday admitted they had not been to church in a while.

Melinda Barnwell, who moved to Pleasant Grove in February, said she had a new perspective on life after she, her four children and her fiance survived the tornado as their house was blown down on top of them. "We're not regular churchgoers," Barnwell said. "We needed our eyes opened."

Jackson, who has preached at Bethel Baptist Church many times over the years because of his friendship with Pastor T.L. Lewis, toured Pratt City the day before and saw up-close the tornado's wrath.

"It has turned churches and homes

into broken matchsticks," he said. "Many were killed, but many more survived because they had heard the warnings.

"The flip side of this crisis is opportunity," he added.

"We derive beauty from the ashes. Our faith will not refrain from the face of tragedy."

Willie Hyde revisits the site of his home in Concord, which was destroyed by the tornado. Hyde walks amid the rubble of his home at the point where he was able to crawl from under the debris.

Alabama Power workers lift a crewman over a jumble of downed trees to complete a repair at the top of this power pole in the Wylam community.

Military men protect damaged areas throughout the area; this scene from Pratt City.

Gov. Robert Bentley at Children's Hospital visits with Pleasant Grove's Curt Grier and his daughter 5-year-old Rachel Grier, who was hurt in the tornadoes when a porch collapsed on them in their basement.

Significant sections of the city of Fultondale may be permanently reshaped by the tornado that ripped through town April 27.

The tornado — the tail end of the devastating Tuscaloosa-to-Birmingham twister — cut a mile-wide swath through the city stretching from the city's southern border with Birmingham to Walker Chapel Road.

Bearing its brunt were the residential neighborhoods of Glendale, Black Creek Station, Fultondale Estates and Lewisburg Gardens and the business district on U.S. 31.

"It was a monster tornado," said Fultondale Police Chief Byron Pigg. "The damage is about as bad as you can find. We were very lucky to escape that without a fatality. I attribute that to the advanced warning. They got to a safe place. It was miraculous that no one was killed."

One major change comes with the severe damage to two large apartment complexes on U.S. 31, Fulton Hill and Fulton Ridge. They have been condemned by the city and residents are moving out.

"The apartment buildings will have to completely come down," Pigg said.

Complicating any attempt to rebuild those apartments is a city-imposed moratorium on apartments. Fultondale Mayor Jim Lowery said the moratorium was imposed because of school crowding in the city.

Also problematic will be trying to figure out how to rebuild in the Glendale neighborhood, one of the city's original communities. Glendale and Fulton Springs combined to form the city.

The neighborhood of small houses was home to the families of coal miners who worked in the area. Wednesday's tornado sent hundreds of century-old oaks crashing into the homes.

Many of the home lots are only 25 to 40 feet wide, making it nearly impossible to build family homes back under modern zoning restrictions, Lowery said. Besides that, several of the homes were vacant, he added. The area is on the sewer system so it makes sense to redevelop it, but it will take creativity to figure out how to do it.

And finally, the city was already in the midst of a long-term redevelopment plan for the business district on U.S. 31, where many businesses were wiped out. The final draft of that plan is due out in 30 to 60 days.

"That plan may be implemented a lot sooner than we expected," Lowery said.

'A call to action'

Nearly a week after the tornado, former Secretary of State Condoleezza Rice, along with golfers Hale Irwin and Tom Watson and radio personalities Tom Joyner and Rickey Smiley, converged on the Red Cross Disaster Relief Center at Scott School in Pratt City to encourage continued care and support for the tornado victims.

The school served as both a donation drop-off site and a place where victims could come for supplies and services, including medical care, counseling services, hot meals, clothing and cleaning supplies.

Rice, who grew up in Birmingham, offered prayers, condolences and support.

"I am obviously here, and we are here, to let people know that we are deeply moved by the tragedy that has struck this great state," she said.

Joyner promised to mobilize his radio audience to come to the storm victims' aid. "We are going to rally our 8 million listeners and have them donate," he said. "We are going to issue a call to action."

Birmingham Mayor William Bell said the almost total loss of the Pratt City neighborhood, where at least 1,000 homes were destroyed, creates an opportunity to look at how to better build that and other areas of the city.

"We're trying to find a silver lining in all of this," Bell said. "I want to rebuild these communities better than they were before."

Pratt City is one of the communities in the city that seem to always be in the path of deadly twisters, the mayor added.

Longtime Pratt City resident Charlette Naylor can attest to that. The April 27 tornado was her third. She survived tornadoes that hit the neighborhood in 1977 and in 1998.

"We have a couple of neighborhoods that have been hit three times in the last 20 years by tornadoes, and they're kind of leery about going back," Bell said.

"This may give us an opportunity to design better communities as we go back and replace these communities."

The devastation in Pratt City brought back horrible memories for Birmingham Police Chief A.C. Roper.

"It reminds me of my deployment to Homestead (Fla.) after Hurricane Andrew," Roper said. "Seeing our citizens with a look of despair and hopelessness is heartbreaking."

As bulldozers, public works trucks and Birmingham police drove through debris-littered streets, weary-eyed residents carried garbage bags containing what little they could save.

Many pitched in to help however they could, some choosing to serve lunch to storm victims and rescue workers.

The Church of the Highlands and the Spoonfed Grill food truck served

Above: Roderick Childress (in green) gets sandwiches as volunteers Lavon Evans, in blue, Edward Jones, in burgundy, and JeSeta Mallory, in red, distribute food and water on Cherry Avenue in Pratt City.

Left: Judy Cook of Concord, who lost her Masters Drive home, is comforted by Chase Spradlin.

Sisters Shannon and Sarah Calcatera, both UAB students, walk through the destroyed Concord community handing out bottled water Saturday morning after the Wednesday tornado. They were volunteers with Hands On Birmingham.

Wendy Early, left, helps Matt Dillon look for things from his house that blew over on the rubble of a neighbor's home. Dillon's wife, Rebecca (not pictured) stayed in the structure on the right during the storm and escaped without harm.

Red Cross volunteer Shirley Gavin Floyd rests on a pile of lumber as she takes a break from sorting through rubble in Pratt City.

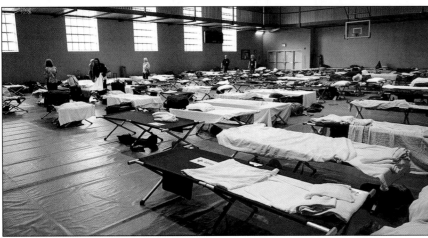

Top left: Volunteers Lena Mekdad, left, and Aisha Abbas sort items at the Salvation Army temporary relief storage site on Industrial Drive.

Top right: Amy Humphries of Hueytown stands on the porch of what was her uncle Joe Wilson's home, just off Concord's Masters Drive.

Above: Red Cross volunteers from across the country set up cots in the Bashinsky Field House at Samford University.

Above right: Tears of sadness and joy were shed throughout the Bethel Baptist Church service held May 1 at Birmingham's Fair Park Arena.

Right: Church pews serve as shelving for items donated to storm victims in the Concord area.

meals at a gas station across the street from Pratt City Fire Station.

Members of Delta Sigma Theta sorority made sandwiches while the Salvation Army and Community Food Bank of Central Alabama handed out bottled water and snacks.

Although clearly grateful for such acts of kindness, many residents questioned what the future held for the storm-swept neighborhoods.

'Got to have glitter'

Six days after the tornado plowed through Concord and killed six of its residents, students returned to Concord Elementary School missing two of their classmates.

Third-grader Lexi Kreider and her big brother, fourth-grader Mikey Kreider, died in the tornado along with their mother, Michelle Kreider.

Many other Concord Elementary students lost their homes.

"We have 15 children whose houses were completely destroyed, and others are just scared to death," Principal David Foster said.

Fourth-grader Cassie Hicks lost her home, but was thankful to come back

to school and see her friends.

"My house is gone," she said. "There's lots of wood, and it's just in a pile."

Children in the younger grades at Concord spent the morning painting pictures about their experiences.

Older children were able to share what they went through with classmates and teachers. Guidance counselor Renae Roszell said the children discussed "heart-wrenching things" as they relived memories of their classmates Lexi and Mikey.

The third-graders made cards in Lexi's memory.

"One little boy said, 'We've got to have glitter,'" Roszell said. "'We've got to have glitter because Lexi sparkled.'"

'Stay strong'

For students at Jackson-Olin High School, about 80 of whom were left homeless by the storm, the tornado hit nine days before the school prom. Many of them lost their prom dresses in the storm.

But thanks to an outpouring of community support, their prom went on as scheduled. And everybody had

something nice to wear to "Midnight in Paris," the prom theme.

Students in Shelby County heard about their dilemma and donated more than 100 dresses and dozens of pairs of shoes for the Jackson-Olin students to choose from.

As word spread around the country, the Shelby County school system alone collected another 3,000 prom dresses.

Spurred on by the morning crew on the "Roy Wood Jr. Show" at radio station 95.7 JAMZ, Men's Wearhouse donated tuxedoes for all the young men, and cosmetology students at Virginia College offered free manicures, pedicures and hair styling to the young ladies.

One donated dress came with a hand-written note from the survivor of another horrific storm.

"I hope you will have a few hours of happiness at your prom," the note said. "I assure you, having survived Katrina, you will make it through this difficult time.

"Stay strong, find the small things to be thankful for, and follow your dreams."

"I assure you, having survived Katrina, you will make it through this difficult time."

Hand-written note attached to a prom dress donated to Jackson-Olin High School students

6:23 p.m.
St. Clair and Calhoun Counties

"This has been so tough. You just can't describe it."

Sandi Mitchell, who lost her uncle in the tornado

Shortly before the tornado hit, high school sweethearts Angie and Al Sanders, along with their daughters Cecily, Cassie and Ciera, sat on the front porch of their Ashville home eating brownies that Angela made earlier that day.

They knew a storm was coming, but they didn't know the gravity of it. Not then.

When the tornado got closer, Al

Sanders gathered his family in the safest place they had, the bathroom.

"It wouldn't have mattered where they were," Angie Sanders' older sister, Lorie Burgess, said. "All that was left of the house was the foundation. Everything in the house was shredded. Everything they had was in tiny pieces."

The twister left Angie dead, Al dying and the three girls hurt badly.

Al and Angie Sanders were among

15 people in St. Clair County who lost their lives in the April 27 tornado.

St. Clair County Emergency Management Agency officials estimated that 1,400 homes in the county were affected by the tornado, including about 300 homes in the hard-hit Shoal Creek Valley area.

Not far from the Sanderses, three generations of the Isbell family — 56-year-old Ronnie Isbell; his 31-year-old daughter-in-law, Tammy Isbell;

Kelly Crawford watches as volunteers salvage belongings from her destroyed house in Shoal Creek Valley near Ashville.

82

A motorist passes through the tornado-ravaged Shoal Creek Valley near Ashville. At least 11 people were killed during a tornado that traveled at least seven miles through the narrow St. Clair County valley.

Goshen Methodist—Example of hope

As victims of the April 27 tornado come to Goshen United Methodist Church outside Piedmont, they tend to tell their stories.

Mike Tyree has heard them.

He hears them when he delivers meals to homes without power and to displaced families in rented houses and hotels.

He nods at the stories, all too familiar, and like his fellow church members, he remembers.

The storms struck close to the church, damaging as many as 50 homes and leaving church secretary Janet Woods without one.

Although many in the church missed the worst of the April 27 tornado outbreak, Tyree and others have been on the other side.

On March 27, 1994, Goshen's Palm Sunday service was interrupted by a sudden power outage and a pelting sound hitting the church's windows. It was debris.

At that moment, an EF4 tornado ripped the roof from the church and slammed it down on a nearly full house of worshippers, collapsing a wall on one side of the church.

By day's end, 20 people had died there.

Goshen became a national focal point for the week after, with Vice President Al Gore visiting the tiny community.

The church eventually was rebuilt a little farther up Alabama 9.

Seventeen years after that tragic Palm Sunday, almost 100 church members got involved in daily volunteer efforts to help the victims of this year's tornadoes.

The church itself became a mini-relief center, filled with food, clothing and household goods for those in need.

"We're here because of the tornado in 1994," Renee Turner, who coordinated Goshen's relief efforts, said. "We rebuilt because of everyone else's donations. We have to be the first responder.

"We have to set the example that good can come from all the heartache," she added. "I'm just proud to be part of such an amazing group that wants to give back."

On April 27, Tyree, now 63, was in his basement with his family and his grandchildren, wondering if the storm would strike Goshen.

On Palm Sunday 1994, he was the church lay leader when the storm struck, pinning him under the roof. He crawled out hugging the carpet, fearing his wife, Linda, and their twin boys were dead. They all survived.

Linda Tyree said she sees victims of the 2011 storms going through the same conflicting emotions that she and her fellow church members experienced 17 years ago.

Survivors have gratitude mixed with guilt — thankful their lives have been spared, yet wondering why.

"That's how we were," she said.

Another longtime church member, Jeanette Griffith, has helped deliver meals to tornado victims. She experienced no storm damage, but her aunt, sister-in-law and a few friends lost their homes, she said.

In 1994, Griffith was pinned under the church roof for about 45 minutes and emerged with cuts and bruises. The woman who had been sitting next to her during the service died.

"It feels like it's happening all over again, anytime the weather gets bad," she said. "It makes you want to take cover.

"I am better than I was right after the storm, since '94," she added. "I used to get so nervous and upset, but I'm handling it better these days."

83

Three members of the Isbell family were laid to rest at Ragland United Methodist Church cemetery. Ronnie Isbell, 56, Tammy Isbell, 31, and Leah Isbell, 7, were three of the hundreds of victims of the tornado outbreak April 27. The crowd overflowed at Usrey Funeral Home in Pell City.

The tornado flattened homes near Ohatchee on Neely Henry Lake.

McDonald Chapel suffered a serious hit from a deadly tornado; one person was killed and several houses were destroyed.

Power crews work to restore power on Eagle Cove Road off Alabama 77 north of Ohatchee. A battered tornado warning siren took a direct hit but still stands. Debris from homes litters the hillside.

and his 7-year-old granddaughter, Leah Isbell — were killed when the tornado hit the assisted-living center Ronnie Isbell owned.

Four residents of the center, housed in two L-shaped, double-wide mobile homes, also died in the storm.

The Isbells lived there along with Tammy Isbell's husband, Kevin, who was not home when the tornado struck. Tammy helped her father-in-law run the facility, caring for the residents and preparing meals.

"This has been so tough," Sandi Mitchell, Ronnie Isbell's niece, said later. "You just can't describe it."

In neighboring Calhoun County, nine were killed, including five in the town of Ohatchee.

One of those was Ruby Douthitt, a nurse who was on her knees praying with her husband when the tornado hit their house. Her husband survived.

Michael and Tina Forrest, also of Ohatchee, were killed after the tornado blew their house into Neely Henry Lake.

He grabbed some debris in the lake and held on until rescue workers could pull him out, but he died the next day in the hospital. Her body was found in the lake the day after the tornado.

Four families, 37 people, one basement

In Shoal Creek Valley, where the tornado traveled at least seven miles through the narrow valley in St. Clair County, 37 people from four families gathered in the basement of the home of Aaron and Kelly Crawford to ride out the storm.

The parents of nine children, the Crawfords opened their home to three other families, including a mother of four who was seven months pregnant.

Although they were safe in the basement, they could hear the rest of the home being lifted from its foundation, Aaron Crawford said.

"The men had to put their weight against the door to keep it from blowing open," he said.

After the storm subsided and the Crawfords realized their home was uninhabitable, they went out into the dark to find somewhere to stay for the night.

The journey began with a two-hour effort to pull their neighbors — a family of 15 — from their collapsed home.

The father, Thomas Carl Lee, was dead, and several of the couple's 13 children were severely injured. Lee died trying to shield one of his children from the debris from the storm.

"They're an awesome family," Aaron Crawford said of the Lees. "He'd been over earlier and we begged him to stay with us."

In the dark, Crawford and others were able to jack up the house and pull out the survivors.

After making sure their neighbors were cared for, the group of 37 made its way through downed power lines and tree limbs in the pitch-black dark to find a safe place for the night.

Robert Preskitt of Eagle Cove Road north of Ohatchee picks through debris thrown into his backyard from the mobile home that once stood next door. A cove of Neely Henry Lake in background is strewn with debris.

Aaron Crawford salvages a cabinet from his destroyed home in Shoal Creek Valley near Ashville.

"We organized a line of people, with older ones holding the children and the men in front looking for power lines," Crawford said. "There was a lot of shock, a lot of numbness. I think that's the body's way of coping."

Time to clean up and pitch in

Among the group was Mercy King, the pregnant mother of four, her husband and their kids, who ran to the Crawfords' home without shoes as the storm approached.

"We didn't have a basement, so I knew if a tornado came, I knew we'd be toast," King said.

They found shoes and jackets at the Crawfords' home and trusted in God as they made their journey, she added.

"It was almost impossible to see because of the darkness and debris, but there was a lot of peace," she said. "We felt the Lord's hand on us."

Eventually, the families decided to stay the night with Gary Boyd, a man who had stayed with them in the basement and whose house was not destroyed by the storm.

They made it to safety, but then had to deal with the aftermath of the storm.

For the Crawfords, that meant finding a place to live.

"Everything normal in our lives is gone," Kelly Crawford said. "But we're surviving with the peace that God gives us."

King, whose home suffered only minor roof damage, said she is trying to help all those who were less fortunate than her family.

"The first step was to get through the storm," she said. "Now, it's time to start cleaning up and support people who need it."

A destroyed house in Shoal Creek Valley near Ashville.

5 a.m. and 5 p.m. Walker County

"This is the hardest we've ever been hit."

Cordova Fire Chief Dean Harbison

Jesse Dutton navigated a maze of downed trees and power lines to a rise overlooking his devastated hometown of Cordova, hit by two tornadoes 12 hours apart. The second storm killed four here.

"Look at the houses destroyed, roofs gone, the whole hillside over there," Dutton said, gesturing to his left, then sweeping his arm across a debris-strewn vista.

"The clinic destroyed. The laundromat gone. The Piggly Wiggly destroyed. The Rebel Queen restaurant gone. The ballpark destroyed."

Walker County Coroner J.C. Poe reported nine known fatalities in Walker County associated with the storm — one in Oakman, four in Cordova, two in the Argo community on U.S. 78 and two in Sipsey.

In Cordova, the dead included Jonathan Doss, 12, and his brother Justin, 10, as well as Annette Singleton, 46, and Jackson Vann Horn, 24.

The first tornado arrived at 5 a.m. April 27, devastating the historic

Few trees are left standing on a hillside in Sipsey where cleanup and recovery continued in the Walker County town in the aftermath of the April 27 tornado outbreak.

downtown, collapsing the brick facades of buildings and tearing off roofs.

It flipped the police mobile command center and downed trees before heading on to Jasper, where it also damaged downtown buildings and downed trees. The deadly second twister arrived about 12 hours later, barreling down a slope and flattening several commercial buildings just south of downtown.

The storm ripped a roof off of the historic home of the town's founder.

It toppled the bell tower of century-old Long Memorial Methodist Church and blew out its stained glass.

It ripped the roof off the town's only grocery and smashed a pharmacy.

It sent hundreds of trees down on homes and power lines.

The morning after, generators and chain saws whined and heavy equipment rumbled, as emergency responders went house-to-house looking for more victims and working to clear the roads.

Dean Harbison, Cordova's fire chief, was directing emergency personnel out of a makeshift headquarters.

The fire station was destroyed and the fire department's mobile command center disintegrated in the tornado's fury.

During the tornado, Harbison and

Messages seeking help painted on a destroyed house in Sipsey. Cleanup and recovery continued in the Walker County town in the aftermath of the April 27 tornado outbreak.

Two people were killed when this double-wide mobile home was hit by a tornado in Sipsey.

The remains of a house and mobile home in Sipsey.

other city officials had to take shelter under City Hall.

"This is the hardest we've ever been hit," he said.

Carol Twilley, her children and their friends were taking medical records out of the rubble of the town clinic operated by her husband, Dr. Scott Twilley.

"It's pretty much a total loss," she said. "We're looking for anything we can salvage right now."

But she was thankful.

"Things can be replaced," she said. "People cannot."

Ronnie Driver, 30, was in a home not far from downtown when the evening tornado hit.

First the air filled with flying debris. Then came a sound like a madly whistling teapot.

Trees started snapping. A trampoline was picked up and thrown into a neighbor's yard.

It lasted about 15 seconds, Driver estimated.

After the tornado passed, he made his way downtown.

"We were the first ones to get here, and it was pretty bad," he said. "It looked unreal, like a movie."

Rob Gurganus, 40, wandered through the scrambled wreckage in rooms of his roofless home, a white-columned mansion built before 1885 by Cordova founder Benjamin Long.

"I was raised in this house," Gurganus said. "The first tornado put a tree on it, the second took the roof."

A well of determination

The same evening tornado that wrecked Cordova dropped down on the Argo community on U.S. 78, killing two residents and smashing seven houses and a business owned by an extended family.

Two days after the storm, on a decimated Walker County hilltop where her ancestors settled in the 1880s, 75-year-old Anne Muse kept repeating a phrase for strength.

"God is able," she said. "God is able."

Half of Sipsey Gone

Mayor Anita Sanders hustled around the Sipsey Community Center, helping orchestrate a homemade relief effort in the off-the-beaten-path town where two died and 50 or 60 families were left homeless after the April 27 tornado.

A dozen men worked outside on seven charcoal grills, flipping burgers and grilling hot dogs.

A dozen women scurried to and from the community center kitchen laying out a spread of food.

Tables in the main room were mounded with donated clothes available for the people who had lost virtually everything.

"We're three miles wide and we lost a mile-and-a-half of it," Sanders said. "But you would not believe the way people have turned out here."

Sipsey was in the path of an extremely powerful tornado that swept across central Walker County, killing nine people, including Sipsey residents Pam Jett, 45, and her husband Junior, 48, whose double-wide mobile home was ripped off its foundation and smashed into pieces 50 feet up a nearby hillside.

Sipsey Fire Chief Justin Hagler said after the storm passed about 5:45 p.m., rescue workers headed for the damage but had to proceed on foot because so many trees were blocking the road.

"It took us about five minutes to find the impact zone," Hagler said.

They were awestruck by the storm's power. The heavy metal frames of trailers were wrapped around trees like neckties. Entire houses vanished.

"There are two-story houses down there we cannot find," Hagler said.

While Sipsey received little media attention, help found its way in. People from neighboring towns streamed in soon after the storm passed through. Anita Walker, director of the Sipsey Elementary School lunchroom, offered up food from the school's cafeteria, and manned the community center kitchen.

All the way from Memphis, Frontier Beverage sent in food and supplies.

And the citizens of Sipsey pitched in any way they could, catching sleep in snatches, Sanders said.

"We're three miles wide and we lost a mile-and-a-half of it."

Sipsey Mayor Anita Sanders

But upon re-entering her tornado-ravaged red-brick home for the first time after storms tore through Walker County, Muse gasped.

"Oh, Jesus."

Sunlight poured through her home's vanished ceiling.

Soggy insulation and shards of glass coated the furniture and floors.

Muse steadied herself as she reached the corner of the kitchen where she had lain on the floor when the tornado ripped off her roof.

The memories raced back.

In the chaos that followed that awful storm, relatives found her sister, Lucille Waters, 89, and Waters' grandson-in-law Wesley Starr, 45, dead.

They lived just yards away from Muse in a double-wide trailer blown apart by the winds.

Hearing screams, the relatives raced to find Muse's daughter, Alondan, 50, and grandson, Alvilonte, 14. They were next door in a modular home also ripped apart. They were sent to Birmingham hospitals with broken bones and head injuries.

"He never puts more on than you can bear," Muse said, her voice welling with emotion. "God is able, but I don't know how much more I can bear."

Muse has borne a lot.

The death and destruction caused by the tornado followed other recent tragedies in her life.

A damaged home in the Walker County community of Argo.

As she picked through the shattered glass of picture frames, she found intact a picture of her two granddaughters, Alondan Turner and Catherine Anne Muse.

The young women died last year along with two other college-age friends in the fire that consumed a Day's Inn in Hoover.

That had been just a month after her husband passed away.

"I've been through a lot," she said. "I can't take it."

Then, after a pause, she spoke from a deeper well of determination.

"But He is able. God is able."

What to do next

Muse was one of seven girls and eight boys reared on Hagler Hill in the Argo community, children of a coal-mining father.

Her brother, T.J. Hagler, 79, was living next door to Muse in the small, cobbled-together home where the family was raised. Hagler spent 27 years in the Army, including stints in Korea and Vietnam, before retiring to Hagler Hill.

On the night of the tornado, he was watching storm coverage on television until the house shook and his TV tumbled off the stand.

Hagler pulled two recliners back from the wall and dove under just as the tornado ripped off his roof. The wall behind him fell forward but was caught by the backs of the recliners, sparing his life.

Two days later, Hagler shook his

"God is able, but I don't know how much more I can bear."

Anne Muse of the Argo community

Anne Muse, 75, at her tornado-damaged home in Walker community of Argo.

head as he looked back at the narrow space where he sheltered, visible through the remains of his shattered house.

"I survived," Hagler said, shaking his head. "God's got plans for me yet."

Muse and her brothers, T.J. and Riley Hagler, 84, along with a dozen other members of the extended family and community volunteers, were at a loss to figure out what to do next.

"I need a car. I need to get down to Birmingham," Muse said, fretting about how she would get to the Red Cross office and to the hospital to be with her daughter and grandson.

There was their sister's funeral to attend to. Insurance agents to reach.

Muse picked up envelopes scattered around the front yard, hoping to find her sister's financial records.

T.J Hagler, looking at two riding lawnmowers buried under rubble, wondered: "How am I going to get the grass cut in the cemetery?"

"Don't you be thinking about small stuff," Riley Hagler bellowed back.

Brought out the best

Muse left Hagler Hill after graduating from high school and settled in New York City. She graduated from New York University, where she met her husband, who worked for Avis Rent-a-Car and ran a car repair business.

They retired to Hagler Hill in 1994 to help raise grandchildren and be close to other kin.

Now much of their community is in tatters.

Another relative on the hill, Jeff Hagler, spent another day trying to recover what equipment he could from his auto-detailing business.

Dozens of cars he was working on were totaled in the storm and his business office was wiped clean to the concrete slab.

His wife, Tonya, and 11-year-old son, Truman, were gathering what clothes,

books and belongings they could find amid the debris that was once their home.

They also were having to contend with outsiders coming in and carting off anything of value.

"People are picking up scrap metal," Jeff Hagler said. "Someone has to stay out here at night just to keep a watch."

But the storms also brought out the best in people.

Whatever racial lines existed before the storm were wiped away in this community, as blacks and whites pitched in to help one another.

A downtown street is deserted in Cordova; all of the buildings have been condemned and will have to be demolished.

Below left: Debris being cleared in downtown Cordova.
Below right: Storm winds twisted this yield sign in Cordova.

"We brought some biscuits and water," said Paulette Murray, who carried an armful of foil-wrapped homemade biscuits to the Haglers.

Murray, her family and friends had cranked up the kitchen using generators, having trekked to Ensley, the closest place they could find fuel. They had set up a generator to run the oxygen machine of elderly relatives and were delivering food they had cooked at their home in nearby Rocky Hollow.

"We're just trying to help anywhere we can," Murray said.

While Muse puzzled over where various belongings had landed, she also worked the phones, talking to far-flung relatives.

There was a report that her daughter's condition was improving. Doctors were bringing her out of heavy sedation gradually, assessing what further surgery she might need.

Then, a call came from her pastor, who was in Birmingham at Children's Hospital, checking on Muse's grandson.

"The pastor called from the hospital," Muse exclaimed. "They told me my baby is moving his hand.

"Oh, God is able!" she said. "God is able!"

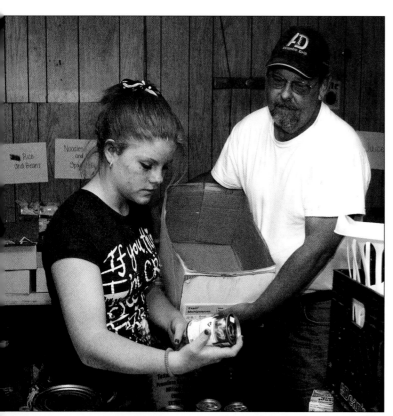

Left: Maggie Benson, 13, helps storm victim Jim Hyche select items in the food pantry at the community center in Cordova. Several teenagers assisted in the distribution of food, clothing and supplies at the center.

Below: John Hudson of Florence (left) and other volunteers carry relief supplies at the community center in Cordova.

Above: A homeowner leaves a large thank-you message in Sipsey. The sign is all that is left; the house is gone.

Below: Volunteers prepare food at the Sipsey Community Center.

2:43 p.m.
Cullman and Marshall Counties

Chris Austin photographed a tornado as it approached and struck downtown Cullman on Wednesday, April 27.

Sonya Nix had just barricaded herself and her employees in a storage room when the April 27 tornado tore into her downtown Cullman consignment shop, Better Than Before.

"I felt a cold blast of air, and the pressure in my ears changed," Nix said as friends and family began boarding up shattered shop windows.

Barely half an hour had passed after the storm subsided before people Nix had never met began asking her how they could help.

"We have some wonderful people in Cullman," she said. "I'm just thankful none of my employees was hurt."

Two Cullman County residents were killed in the tornado, however.

Keenan Jonathan Sullivan, 20, died after a tree fell on the car in which he was a passenger, and 68-year-old Lloyd Winford Harris perished after getting caught in the storm that hit the Simcoe community.

The tornado that tore through Nix's consignment shop also ripped half the roof off the Cullman County Courthouse and heavily damaged the First Baptist Church-Cullman.

Downtown railroad tracks were covered with storm debris, and trees that once made up the downtown skyline were all but leveled. Windows were blown out of every building within two blocks of the courthouse.

Splintered trees, bricks ripped from walls, toppled signs and a crumpled cellphone tower littered the streets.

The three-story First Baptist Church lost one of its back corners, the roof of a newly built fellowship center was heavily damaged, and three stained-glass windows were blown out of the 60-year-old sanctuary.

Residents of Pearson Street in Fairview at their tornado shelter as Alabama was hit hard by storms Wednesday, April 27.

Aerial view of tornado-ravaged downtown Cullman.

Shane Hale, his sister and Elton Hale look at a video of the tornado that hit their neighborhood.

"The children's worship center is totally annihilated," Brian Witcher, minister of music at the church, said.

Standing near a pile of shattered stained glass that once bore the image of Christ on the cross, Pastor Edwin Hayes said community members would pull together to help each other out in their time of need.

"God's people will come together," Hayes said as people pitched in to make repairs to the sanctuary. "God's people are at their best when circumstances are at their worst."

The people of downtown Cullman seemed eager to prove him correct.

As rain continued to pour down, a woman circled the streets in a pickup truck handing out bottles of water. And those whose businesses were less heavily damaged opened their doors to let strangers come in out of the rain.

Help also came from outside Cullman.

On the Friday following the tornado outbreak, Auburn football coach Gene Chizik, who had been in New York

City the night before to watch Cam Newton and Nick Fairley go in the first round of the NFL Draft, came back to Alabama to aid tornado victims in Cullman and Pleasant Grove.

Two busloads of Auburn players, coaches and administrative personnel cleaned churches, visited distribution centers and talked to survivors.

"Our message was hope," Chizik said.

'As good a people as you will ever meet'

Cutting a swath as wide as three-quarters of a mile, the tornado entered northwest Marshall County just after 3 p.m., packing winds of about 190 mph.

It had come out of Cullman County and southeastern Morgan County, gaining strength as it entered Marshall County around Hog Jaw Road.

From the top of their home on Marshall County Road 1815 west of Arab, Brian and David Box saw the tornado heading toward them, bobbing like a yo-yo.

Up and down. Up and down. On the ground, then up in the air, then back on the ground.

Looking through David's cell-phone camera, the tornado appeared to be two small funnels. Suddenly, the funnels came together, forming one large tornado that looked fearsome to them — at least three or four miles wide, in their view.

David's cell phone told the time: 3:08 p.m.

Top: An Alabama State Trooper walks past a damaged county vehicle in downtown Cullman shortly after a tornado hit the area.

Center: A cell tower in Fairview in Cullman County that was hit by the tornado.

Bottom: Elton Hale walks past his house on Pearson Street in Fairview in Cullman County.

The tornado created swirls of pine trees and threw them like match sticks.

The storm churned toward Mat Morrow and Ruth roads in the Ruth community, where cattle and a trailer park were among the casualties.

"I saw horses and cows flying," said Christina Hyde, a resident of the trailer park. "You can't even tell there was a park there."

A storage shed with farm equipment was splattered, hurling the large machinery 10 to 20 yards, by the estimate of the National Weather Service in Huntsville.

Farther east, on Mount Oak and Frontier roads, homes were lifted off their foundations. A home on Frontier Road, just north of Arab, contained nine members of the Hallmark family. Five were killed.

The victims were Ann and Phillip Hallmark; their son and daughter-in-law, Shane and Jennifer Hallmark; and their grandson, Jayden Hallmark.

They were among nine family members who huddled together in a bathroom when the EF4 tornado packing 170-mph winds swept through a pasture and slammed into Phillip and Ann Hallmarks' home on Frontier Road. The other four survived.

When the storm hit, it carried the family over a ravine, and the victims were found about 200 yards from the house.

"They were as good a people as you will ever meet," Deborah Head, a neighbor of the Hallmark family, said. "They were just kind, good people."

The site of the Hallmark home was a grim, sober reality.

A family Bible lay on the ground, slightly muddied.

A baby's toy block set was covered by a fallen oak tree.

Next to a flipped pick-up truck was another that was folded into an upside-down V.

> "They were as good a people as you will ever meet. They were just kind, good people."
>
> **Deborah Head, neighbor of Phillip and Ann Hallmark, who were killed along with three other members of their family.**

Top: National Guardsmen patrol downtown Cullman.

Center: Aerial view of tornado-ravaged downtown Cullman.

Left: Damaged homes near downtown Cullman.

A large piece of metal — 10 to 12 feet long — was wrapped around a utility pole below where the pole had been snapped by the winds.

Dozens of large oak trees were piled on top of each other.

But what was left of the front yard was immaculately manicured, right down to the flowers meticulously planted into a bed at the base of one tree that refused to fall.

"They had it so pretty," another neighbor, Beth Casey, said. "They kept their yard so beautiful."

Kenny Casey, Beth Casey's former husband, was in a nearby storm shelter when the tornado hit and was one of the first people to reach the victims.

When he noticed Shane and Jennifer Hallmark's 6-year-old daughter, Ari, moving, Casey scooped her up and carried her to safety.

"You've got to do what you've got to do," Casey said. "You don't want to go over there, but you have to.

"It would be a little different if you didn't know them, but when you know them . . ."

'Just putting others above yourself'

The week after the tornado, contributions continued pouring in at the Ruth Volunteer Fire Department.

Bill Cash and Kevin Long were among several employees of Sandvir Medical Solutions in Arab who brought in 250 boxed barbecue dinners for victims and emergency workers.

The company's employees prepared and delivered more than 1,100 meals to Holly Pond, Hulaco, Ruth and other areas.

Aerial view of tornado-ravaged downtown Cullman.

Above: Residents look over damage in Fairview in Cullman County.

Left: Workers try to salvage items from Cullman Florist in downtown Cullman after the April 27 tornado.

Tim and Danielle Dodd of Decatur pulled up to the station to unload donated diapers and other items that groups had brought to Ryan School in Morgan County to disburse to victims.

The Dodds, who are members of the Somerville Baptist Church, also delivered meals to storm victims.

"Really, just putting others above yourself," Tim Dodd explained why the couple volunteered to help. "I don't really know another way to say it."

"We wish we could do more," Danielle Dodd added. "There's such a magnitude of needs."

Ruth volunteer firefighter Dewalt Willis said the department sawed trees and searched for people for a day after the storm and later coordinated food distribution.

"We lost friends and had devastation to friends," Willis said. "But everyone's been remarkable. We're doing well. We're just trying to check on everyone."

Later that afternoon, Emily Hammond and her daughter, Madison, 2, left the department and headed for Frontier Road, where the five Hallmark family members were killed.

With help from her daughter, Hammond erected five small crosses in the front yard where the Hallmarks' home stood a week earlier.

The simple wood crosses, adorned with colorful ribbons, stood in stark contrast to the surrounding devastation.

"It's just touching to walk out here where an entire family lost their lives," Hammond said.

"God's people are at their best when circumstances are at their worst."

Pastor Edwin Hayes of First Baptist Church–Cullman

Debris lies near the Cullman County Courthouse (left) and First Baptist Church in downtown Cullman.

Words Can't Explain

On May 5, the funerals were held for the Hallmarks — Phillip, 56; his wife Ann, 54; their son Shane, 37; Shane's wife, Jennifer, 31; and 17-month-old Jayden, Phillip and Ann's grandson.

Brother Jeff Rowan, who officiated, told the story of Jayden's mother, Regina Hallmark, phoning Ann Hallmark as the tornado headed to Ruth.

With their pillows ready, said Ann, the family planned to ride out the storm in a bathroom.

As the choir sang "Amazing Grace," five caskets rolled one after another out of Union Hill First Congregational Methodist Church in Arab.

Outside waited five hearses for transportation to Arab Memorial Cemetery. Of all the images from the deadly tornadoes of April 27, none could be more heart-wrenching than this.

"Folks," said Brother Jeff Rowan, who officiated the service, "words can't explain it."

The family had been together at Phillip and Ann Hallmark's house on Frontier Road just north of Arab. They were keeping their grandchildren, including Jayden and his twin sister, Julie.

Julie, Rowan said, was recovering well.

Shane and Jennifer Hallmark, knowing the storm was approaching, left their newly-constructed house in Ruth to be with their 6-year-old daughter, Ari, who was also with the grandparents. Ari was not seriously injured.

As about 500 people, including Arab Mayor Gary Beam, filled every seat inside the church, the overwhelming question lingered: Why?

Why were there five caskets — all with red roses, except Jayden's, which had white roses — lined at the front of the sanctuary?

Why was this family so devastated?

Why did the tornado have to be so powerful and hit so hard?

Rowan and Brother Sherman Bailey, who also officiated, referred frequently to the Bible and the lifelong suffering of Job.

"If a man dies, will he live again?" Bailey said, quoting Job 14:14.

The answer lies in Job 19:25.

"I know that my Redeemer lives," Bailey said, reading the verse.

Jennifer Hallmark's mother, Susan Garmany, read a poem she had written several months ago.

"Do not hold on to the hurt of this world," the poem read. "It will only make you sad."

But a life in Heaven, the poem said, "will make you glad."

Rowan told of a phone call Regina Hallmark — Jayden's mother — made to Ann Hallmark.

She called with a warning of the approaching storm, and Ann replied that they had their pillows ready and were seeking shelter in the bathroom.

Then Rowan asked the congregation: "Do you have your pillows ready?"

Caskets of members of the Hallmark family who died in the tornado that struck the Ruth community are taken out to waiting hearses following the funeral at Union Hill First Congregational Methodist Church in Arab.

Buck Island subdivision near Guntersville Airport, across the lake from Guntersville State Park Lodge, suffered serious damage.

Kyler Gosch looks for family photos in the wreckage of his grandmother Daryln Johnson's home in Arab's Ruth community.

Clockwise from top: Two residents hug on Frontier Road in Ruth. A whole family was killed at this site.

Debbie Sherman holds her cats she found in her destroyed mobile home at Ruth Trailer Park in Arab.

A devastated Russell Nesmith looks at what is left of his body shop on U.S. 231 South in Arab.

Damage at the marina near the bridge that leads into Guntersville on U.S. 431.

6:19 p.m.
DeKalb and Jackson Counties

At least 33 people died in DeKalb, 200 injured as twister cut 25-mile path

DeKalb County rescue workers and law enforcement spent days after the April 27 tornado outbreak searching for the dead and injured. In the first two days they had pulled 33 lifeless bodies from the rubble.

The tornado carved a path northeast at least 25 miles long from Grove Oak to Ider, injuring an estimated 200, said DeKalb County Sheriff Jimmy Harris.

Along the twister's path, hundreds of homes and businesses were damaged or destroyed, said Alabama state trooper Lt. George Thorpe.

A countywide curfew was put in place to keep gawkers and potential looters away, authorities said. County residents and businesses slowly regained electricity over a period of days after the storm.

Among the hardest hit areas was Rainsville.

The walls of the civic center blew out

Angela Wigley talks about the path of a tornado in Rainsville. Her damaged house is at left.

when the tornado struck about 6:15 p.m. Two empty school buses parked in the center's parking lot were picked up and tossed 50 and 100 yards, across Alabama 35. All that was left of one bus was the chassis. The Huddle House and a credit union on that highway were wiped off their foundations and other businesses severely damaged.

Plainview High School, which is next to the civic center, also was hit by the tornado.

Ginger Graham, a special needs teacher at the school, pulled books from amid the debris that once was the special needs resource room. She was worried about the students.

"We don't know if our students are alive or dead," Graham said.

Search and rescue workers spent much of the day looking for missing people and sifting through debris. The death toll had climbed from 30 on Thursday morning to 36 by late afternoon. State officials later revised that number down to 33.

"So much devastation. So many deaths. It's unreal," said Sheriff Harris.

The state Emergency Medical Agency sent a temporary morgue and freezer to DeKalb County.

Many bodies had no identification. Some were thrown from houses, so it was uncertain where some of the people were before the storm, Harris said.

Among the dead was a family of

Teacher Ginger Graham salvages books from a resource room at Plainview High School in Rainsville.

four — a mother, father and two young children — on DeKalb 85 in the central part of the county.

At least three people were killed off Marshall Road in Rainsville, including a man and woman blown 50 to 100 yards out of their mobile home into a field. Homes were leveled or blown off their foundations along that road.

"I don't know what the crap came through here, but it was evil," said Daniel Berry as he stood by the pile of debris that was once his home on Marshall Road.

Berry wasn't home when the tornado hit. But his wife, brother-in-law Chris Hanenburg and a friend of Hanenburg's were inside.

Hanenburg said trees had been blown down around his house in the Macedonia community in a Wednesday morning storm. He said he had gone with his friend to check on his sister, who was sleeping when they arrived, just before the tornado struck. "If I hadn't gotten her up, we'd be talking differently," he said.

The three ran into the basement of

A damaged truck is decorated in graffiti near Rainsville.

A man carries a tattered American flag from the damaged area of Rainsville.

the house, and were trapped inside about 15 or 20 minutes by the debris piled on top.

Inside Victory Baptist Church a few doors down, a group huddled together in the fellowship hall praying when the tornado hit. "It was rolling over the church like a fog with debris swirling around," said deacon Calvin Thomas.

Hilda Clines, who was praying with Thomas, said, "When the roof came off it felt like it was going to suck us out."

Thomas helped remove the body of one man who was killed when the twister threw him from his mobile home that had sat behind the church before it was blown away. The body of the man's wife was found about 50 yards beyond where her husband's body was found.

Thomas and other church members loaded up pews and other items to store in a dry place because the tornado blew the walls of the church sanctuary out. The top of the steeple also was gone, and they don't know where it landed.

Many residents picked through debris looking for personal items.

Mark Wigley, an independent truck driver, had four of his tractors damaged along with half the top floor of his home ripped off. He and his wife had just gone next door to a neighbor's home who had a basement when the storm hit.

"The good Lord was looking out after us," Wigley said. "We can replace all of this junk."

Calvin Thomas stands near where he pulled a body from the wreckage of a mobile home in Rainsville. Three people died in the immediate area of the mobile home.

A dog is tied to the debris from a destroyed house near Rainsville.

Chris Hanenburg looks at the remains of his sister's house in Rainsville. He and two other people were briefly trapped in the basement but were not injured.

Jackson County

On the day after the storms, Victor Manning, the director of the Jackson County Emergency Management Agency, stood on the courthouse square in Scottsboro and tried to describe what the tornadoes had done.

There was debris on Sand Mountain, mounds and mounds of it strewn on highways and hills. At the base of the mountain in Bridgeport, a 13-year-old boy was dead.

Motorists from Huntsville, Decatur and elsewhere poured into the county, trying to find gasoline in Stevenson and Bridgeport, where there was still power.

There were so many injuries from the storms that "the ambulances were running crazy," Manning said.

The scene was almost overwhelming.

"It's amazing," Manning said. "It really is, just the amount of debris. I really can't explain it."

Here was one way to describe it: On Alabama 117, the highway that runs from Stevenson to Ider, from the north side of Sand Mountain to the south side, there was a house.

One part of the house was on one side of the highway. The other part of the house was on the other side of the highway.

Typical damage, Manning said.

Here was another way to describe it: Five days after the storms, the communities of Higdon and Flat Rock were still determining the impact.

Higdon and Flat Rock are in the farthest northern reaches of Sand Mountain. It is an area so embedded in tradition that many residents rely on the main grocery store in the area, Dobbins Supermarket in Bryant, for information.

Five days after the storms, the news remained grim. Out on Jackson 95, site of the worst damage on the northern part of the mountain, National Guardsmen drove Humvees past the blasted-out remains of chicken houses and trailers.

Before turning onto Jackson 95, the Humvees drove past Tommy Anderson's log-cabin style home. His roof had been blown off when the tornado passed through around 6 p.m. on April 27.

In his front yard, some of his brothers discussed funeral plans for a cousin who'd been killed by the tornado.

"I heard they were going to bury (her) on Wednesday," one of the brothers said.

Their cousin and her husband lived on Jackson 95.

"They went to check on their daughter's home," said Danny Anderson, a concrete factory worker in Ringgold, Ga. "They thought the storm was letting up."

But the storm had not let up.

"And the tornado had killed them while they were at their daughter's home," Danny Anderson said. "It blew the house away."

The day before, a Sunday, there had been a funeral for a 23-year-old resident of Bryant who died when a tornado hit Tuscaloosa. She was one month shy of graduating from the University of Alabama, said a woman who attended the funeral.

There would be more funerals in the coming days.

"One (man) lost his mom and dad," said a woman who works at the supermarket in Bryant. "They found them, but they were not able to have the funeral. They were waiting for the power to come on at the funeral home."

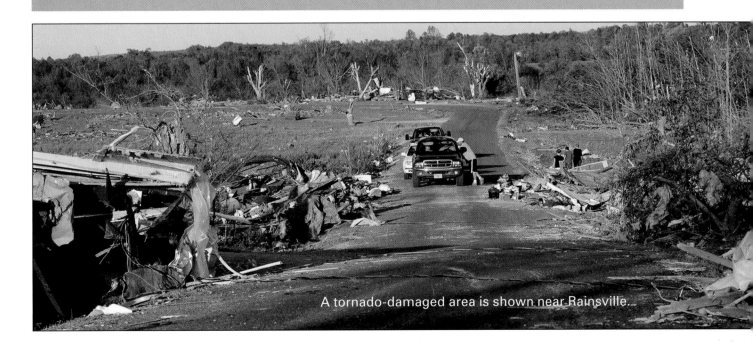

A tornado-damaged area is shown near Rainsville.

The path of a tornado is shown in Rainsville. A body was found in this field after the person was blown out of a mobile home.

In Pisgah, the tornadoes followed each other as if guided by rails, three times over 10 terrifying hours, straight at the little cluster of homes where Joseph Wayne Haney and his relatives lived.

The first crushed Haney's wife, Kathy, to death under a piano. The second twisted menacingly overhead but didn't touch down. The third, a true monster, blew the neighborhood to pieces, killing two more of his kin.

On a day that sowed heartbreak throughout the South, this close-knit family received more than its share of the sky's rage.

"It came back," Haney said, blinking back tears outside a funeral home just days afterward. "It came back the same path, and it killed more."

In Pisgah, like elsewhere, it happened with blinding speed.

Haney was asleep in the living room recliner when his wife, Kathy Gray Haney, woke him.

"She said, 'I think there's a tornado,'" Haney said, "and just as she said the word 'tornado,' it hit us."

Their mobile home heaved into the air and slammed into a line of trees. Their piano landed on the couple, and the rest of the house collapsed on top of it. The family Bible landed next to them.

As the wind screamed, Haney said, he wrapped his arms around his wife's legs and tried to pull her to him.

"She said, 'Honey, I love you, and I'm hurting,'" Haney said.

The week was supposed to be a joyous one for the Haneys and their extended family. Their niece, Whitney Lawhorn, was getting married, and the whole family was invited.

The Haneys themselves had been married 23 years. They met at a dance at the VFW hall and tied the knot just six months later.

Haney, now 45 and known to everyone as just Wayne, was something of a ne'er-do-well back then, he said. But with her smile and her twinkling brown eyes, Kathy straightened him out.

Kathy, 46, liked to take walks in the woods, dig for wild ginseng and collect Indian arrowheads, said her sister, Peggy Lawhorn. She played piano at New Hermon Baptist Church until a stroke last year paralyzed her left arm.

"She'd do anything for you anytime she could," Whitney Lawhorn said. "She didn't care who you were, she wanted to talk to you."

The family was close, Peggy Lawhorn said, with a half-dozen Grays and their spouses all living in a cluster of homes within a half mile of each other on the verdant northern edge of a plateau known as Sand Mountain.

The damaged Rainsville Civic Center.

Brothers Herschel (left) and Norman Kilgore salvage canned goods from their sister's home in Rainsville.

David Martin looks at the remains of his bedroom in Rainsville. He injured his back when the tornado hit.

Above: People look at a destroyed building in Rainsville.

Right: The flooded foundation is all that remains of a destroyed house in Rainsville.

"It came back the same path, and it killed more."

Joseph Wayne Haney

The mountain itself bears much of the blame for what happened April 27, said Richard Lawhorn, Haney's brother-in-law. Jutting 900 feet above the Tennessee River, the flat-topped mountain practically scrapes the bottom clouds of eastward-moving storms.

"It all gets swirled up and comes tearing over the bluff," Richard Lawhorn said.

Of the more than 300 dead from the storms, 33 were in Alabama's northeast corner, much of which is perched on Sand Mountain.

Richard Lawhorn was the first to get to Haney's collapsed mobile home. As he neared the wreckage, he could hear Haney shouting for help. But there was no sound from Kathy.

The family used a tractor with a front-loader attachment to lift the debris. It took 90 minutes for an ambulance crew to pick its way through the fallen trees, and another 90 minutes to get Haney back to the hospital.

Suddenly a second twister materialized, coiling like a snake in the turbulent sky. But it didn't touch down, passing a little to the north of Pisgah.

Then, at 4:30 p.m., another monstrous funnel appeared. It crashed through the trees and obliterated the house of Kathy's great-uncle, Herbert

Satterfield, 90, and his wife, Ann, who was in her 70s.

When the wind settled down, there was nothing left of the house but a few cracked cinder blocks and shattered pieces of floor.

On the following Saturday, the family buried Kathy in the cemetery of Friendship Baptist Church. Chain saws buzzed in the distance. Smoke from burning debris wafted over the graves.

The wedding was postponed. The judge who was supposed to have performed the marriage lost his own son in a tornado in Tuscaloosa.

As the last flowers were piled on Kathy's grave, family members embraced, then headed home to resume the cleanup.

"It doesn't seem right that one family should get hit twice," Richard Lawhorn said. "But at least we've got each other to get through it."

Aluminum sheeting is wrapped around power lines near Rainsville.

Church members salvage pews from Victory Baptist Church in Rainsville. A wall was knocked out of the sanctuary and outbuildings were destroyed.

5:30 p.m.
Hale and Bibb Counties

The skies had darkened and the rain had started to come down hard as Hale County Sheriff Kenneth Ellis drove out to his mother's home on County Road 18 in Sawyerville.

Ellis wanted to make sure his mother and other relatives were "buckled in" for the tornado that was roaring their way.

He was two miles from the house when he saw the top of the tornado.

"My cousin called me a second or two after it hit the house, just hollering for help," he said.

About a mile away from his mother's home, the storms had left so much debris on the road that Ellis and his deputy had to take off on foot.

Once there, they pulled Ellis' mother, his sister, his niece and cousin from the rubble.

The storm destroyed his 78-year-old mother's home, which she built in 1973.

Several other homes in Hale County were also destroyed.

"It looked like somebody dropped a bomb in some areas," the 55-year-old Ellis said. "It looked like the storm stayed on the ground a pretty good while."

Ellis saw to it that his diabetic

The tornado that ravaged much of central Alabama left its mark on Bibb County. Especially hard hit was the community of Eoline.

Emma Royal looks through household items with her grandson Tysen Hamilton, 2, at the Greensboro Recreation Center. The center provided food and clothing and household items for storm victims.

mother, who had just had stents put in her heart, had medical attention following the late-afternoon storm.

After that, the second-term sheriff didn't get to see his family again until 2 the next morning. He was busy helping other families.

Six people died in the tornado, including four from Ellis' hometown of Sawyerville. He knew them all.

The sheriff credits the help of everyone — including volunteers, the fire department, Hale County Emergency Medical Services and others — for working as a group and helping the community through the tragedy.

People continue to call, offering to donate items and volunteer their help.

"We are alive," Ellis said. "We are fine. We will rebuild somehow."

In the meantime, Ellis still has to work on one request from his mother, who was glad he found her purse in the rubble.

"The only thing she still has us looking for is her mother's picture," he said. "We still haven't found that."

Neighbors help neighbors in Bibb County

As the tornado ripped through adjoining Bibb County, nearly a dozen people — some from nearby mobile homes — sought cover inside the bathroom at the Eoline Volunteer Fire Department on Highway 82.

The walls crumbled around them,

and the two fire trucks were destroyed.

One girl emerged with a broken arm and another girl had a broken hand. Everyone else was OK.

"That's what saved them, them being in the bathroom," volunteer Fire Chief Jarred "Peanut" Kornegay said.

Twelve homes, three businesses and the greenhouse at the Bibb County Career Academy were destroyed; another 21 homes and a building at the Bibb County Career Academy received major damage.

Ricky Smith, a logger from Brent, died after the car that carried him and his nephew was blown off U.S. 82. His nephew survived.

Wayne Hayes, EMA director for Bibb County, estimated that 12 to 15 families needed long-term housing assistance.

The hardest-hit areas were the communities of Pondville, off Highway 25; Red Eage, south of West Blocton; and Eoline on U.S. 82, between Centreville and the Tuscaloosa County line, he said.

Like recovery scenes across the state, neighbors pitched in to help neighbors throughout Bibb County.

At Eoline Baptist Church, next door to the destroyed volunteer fire house, people set up a food station and doled out hot meals for at least a week after the storms.

Many residents and power crews also found satisfying meals at the Twix 'n' Tween Restaurant on Walnut Street in Centreville, where the buffet and pork barbecue are popular.

"A lot of people didn't want (fast food) sandwiches," general manager Jackie Wilson said. "They wanted a solid meal."

The lights at the restaurant went out on April 27, and they were back on by 6 a.m. the next day. Thirty minutes later, breakfast was served.

"By lunchtime, everyone was calling and wanted to know if we were open," Wilson said.

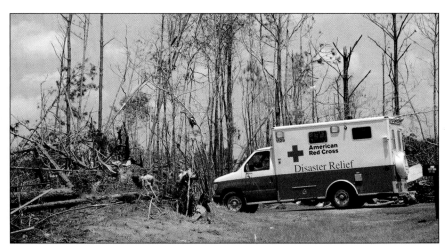

An American Red Cross emergency response vehicle checks on residents affected by the storm in Sawyerville.

112

The only motel in Bibb County, the Winwood Inn in Brent, also became a hub of activity as mostly Alabama Power Co. crews and out-of-state power crews set up temporary lodging.

Some families affected by the storm also stayed at the 42-room motel, which real estate agent Steve Edmonds helps runs with his family.

One family that had been renting a home that was destroyed in the storms stayed at the motel.

When school officials told Edmonds about their situation, he agreed to let the family have several nights for free.

"It's just the time where you have to help," said Edmonds, whose father bought the inn in 1969. It's been in their family ever since.

Edmonds, who lives in Tuscaloosa and also runs the Twix 'n' Tween in Centreville, said the destruction in Eoline was incredible.

"There's a path of destruction," he said. "It's not a wide path like Tuscaloosa is. But where that storm hit it, it destroyed everything in sight."

Dennis Duncan, principal at Bibb County Career Academy, is amazed that the storm that hit Eoline didn't do more damage to his heavily-wooded campus, which lost about 100 pine and hardwood trees.

"Our campus sits up on a hill, and this time of year, you are not able to see our school from (Alabama) Highway 5," Duncan said. "You can now."

The school, halfway between West Blocton and Brent, has three buildings for students.

The building that houses the automotive, forestry and welding classes suffered significant damage, Duncan said. The greenhouse that students finished building in the spring was destroyed.

"It's gone," Duncan said. "There are pieces of it in trees."

Russell Weeden, director of the Emergency Management Agency in Hale County, said 70 homes were destroyed, 150 homes had minor to major damage, and 100 vehicles were destroyed. Most of the destroyed homes were in Sawyerville.

He said the three-quarter-mile-wide tornado was on the ground for 24.5 miles. It hit the area around 5:45 p.m.

There were six fatalities and 40 people were taken to the hospital with injuries. Several of the 40 injured lived in mobile homes and were injured after being thrown from their homes during the storm.

After the tornado hit, the Hale County EMA set up a mobile hospital in the parking lot of the Sawyerville Grocery. The EMA workers' job was to make sure the severely injured received immediate medical attention before being transferred to major hospitals

By the day after the storm, though, there was no longer a need for the mobile hospital, and EMA workers turned it into a mobile kitchen, where they organized the delivery of nearly 6,000 hot meals over the next two weeks.

Their biggest day was Sunday after the storm, when they served more than 800 meals to residents and workers who were helping with the storm's aftermath, Weeden said.

Ten state forestry trucks were used to deliver meals across the county.

"We called it our own meals on wheels," Weeden said.

A cross was place at the entrance to a home destroyed by the tornado in Sawyerville.

American Red Cross disaster relief emergency response vehicle drivers Suzanne Paganelli and Pam Blum, right of Columbus, Ohio, plate food for Sawyerville residents affected by the storm.

8:12 p.m.
Elmore and Tallapoosa Counties

In Eclectic, Nancy Myers walked out of her 5-year-old home below a hill where 11 mobile homes made up a park named Myers Country Acres.

The power was out and her cataract-repaired eyes were overwhelmed by a pitch black night.

Each potential step was littered with tornado debris — most of it the remains of mobile homes she and her husband, Billy Ray Myers, owned. They were shredded by what the National Weather Service declared an EF4 tornado.

The killer storm plowed through Elmore, Tallapoosa and Chambers counties April 27, its winds whipping up to 170 miles per hour as it swelled to a half-mile wide. Six people died in the chaos of its power, including four who lived in two of Myers' homes on Middle Road.

"There's not a dark any darker than a night with no stars and Alabama's power is out for miles," Myers said. "Me being a little old country girl, I'm thinking if I can get to my car door and open the door the light will come on. All across the hill there were people moaning and groaning and hollering for help. This was their little family park. ... You can recognize the voices, but you can't get to them. There was nothing you could do. It was awful."

She could not see the devastation at the time, but the neighborhood Myers once took pride in for being neat, clean and family friendly — a place she said people wanted to live — was a hazardous field of scattered memories that marked the wake of the sinister twister.

Ten minutes after the tornado chopped countless pine trees into kindling and destroyed many of the homes, Myers said she saw flashlights and heard voices: first responders already searching along her street.

As they struggled to inch south through the tangled, twisted mess, Dan Avant, a 58-year-old Vietnam veteran, began his own search-and-rescue mission, according to his neighbor, 60-year-old Eloise Josey.

Avant first checked on Josey, and could hear people calling for help. He managed to work his way through utter destruction, including downed power lines that snaked through the rubble, as he searched for the injured.

Damage remains from tornadoes that swept through the area on April 27 by Middle Road and Auction Barn Road in Elmore County.

Damage from tornadoes that swept through the area on April 27, by Middle Road and Auction Barn Road in Elmore County.

Josey and her 63-year-old husband, Mason Josey, had huddled in the central hallway of their house where they lived for 37 years. They braced as the tornado devoured what Josey said was a 1,500 square-foot addition on the back of their home. The winds pounded the front portion of their home, leaving substantial damage. It even ripped up an electric fence, freeing their donkey and five goats.

In the immediate aftermath, Josey opened her door to the injured, using her living room as an emergency holding area. Three children and two adults would make it to her carpet as they bandaged wounds that would require surgeries.

They sat scattered inside the home until rescuers could reach them 40 minutes after the tornado had passed through, Josey said.

"We had several wounded children in here and I think that's what stuck with people," Josey said. "The emergency people told us they couldn't get in here. ... We didn't know what to do. But they said because of what he

did and we had them down here, he probably saved some lives because they were able to get to them faster."

Inevitably, as Avant worked through the neighborhood he discovered the dead, including Josey's next-door neighbors Martha Ann Myers, 67, and Melissa Ann "Missy" Myers Gant, 43. The mother and daughter were thrown 50 feet from their trailer and found still clutching each other.

Candice Abernathy, 23, was killed after the tornado destroyed her mother's mobile home, her body found in the roadway next to a pile of debris about 100 feet away. Her 5-year-old niece, Kammie Abernathy, was found dead on the other side of the road

about 150 feet away.

Myers said their mother suffered brain damage after she was slung into a ditch. She now speaks like a child.

A few American flags were placed near spots where the dead were found.

"Any time I feel sorry for myself I can look at that pasture and know I'm very fortunate," Josey said. "God blessed me. Maybe it was for the reason to help save those kids. It's horrible. ... I don't think it's hit everybody yet, but it's hard."

The tornado touched down along Elmore 209 near Meadowview Drive as a small storm and began snapping off trees.

Mount Hebron Church of Christ on Mount Hebron Road in Elmore County. The church was a center for food, water and supplies for the survivors of the tornadoes.

But it grew rapidly, tearing up homes in Dexter, tearing through the mobile home park, and then moving on to destroy more homes and businesses, two churches and an agricultural nursery.

Crossing Lake Martin south of the Highway 63 bridge, the storm heavily damaged many homes around the Wyndermere area. By now the storm was a quarter-mile wide and growing, eventually to an estimated half-mile wide, demolishing homes and rolling vehicles in its path.

It crossed U.S. 280 just east of Dadeville, damaging more homes and businesses in that area, then crossed into western Chambers County where

Mount Hebron East Baptist Church is flattened.

it destroyed at least one home before ending north of Chambers 51.

Damage from tornadoes that swept through the area.

Hope rising from tragedy

Help came almost as soon as the deadly storms finally went silent.

Neighbors pitching in to help neighbors.

Strangers rolling up their sleeves to help strangers.

And out of the tragedy rose hope.

"We're going to get through this because the people of Alabama are resilient," Gov. Robert Bentley said the day after Alabama's worst natural disaster in generations. "They care about each other.

"We're going to get through this, and we're going to come out better on the other side."

Already, thousands of Alabamains and others from outside the state were proving the governor right.

Church groups collected and distributed bottled water and baby wipes for those left homeless.

Restaurants grilled hamburgers and smoked barbecue to serve to the storm victims and rescue workers.

Cleanup crews cut sawed trees and sorted through the debris.

Within two days, President Barack Obama was in Tuscaloosa to offer comfort and pledge his support.

"We go through hard times, but no matter how hard we may be tested, we maintain our faith and we look to each other to make sure that we're supporting each other and helping each other," the president said.

"I'm sure that spirit is going to continue until this city is all the way back."

The Rev. Jesse Jackson and comedian Bill Cosby soon followed. So did actor Charlie Sheen and singer Lance Bass, NFL legend Brett Favre and NBA players DeMarcus Cousins and Eric Bledsoe.

Country-music musicians Hank Williams Jr., Sara Evans and the group Alabama — all of whom have close ties to the state — teamed up to put together a nationwide telethon on CMT cable network to raise money for tornado relief efforts throughout the Southeast.

"What we're talking about here is the worst natural disaster in the history of the state," Williams said. "I said, 'We've got to do something.'"

Rivals became friends.

Auburn fan Warren Tidwell of Opelika helped create a Toomer's for Tuscaloosa page on Facebook to raise money and coordinate relief efforts for those who wanted to help their Iron Bowl rivals.

"Helping with the rescue and people in need is what you do," Tidwell said. "Football only goes so far. This is what you do."

Volunteers signed up by the thousands.

Utility workers in Hackleburg work from bucket trucks to restring and reconnect power lines.

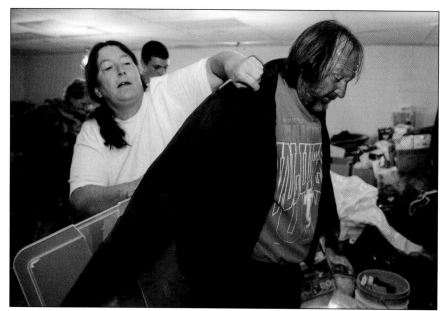

Mary Williams (left) helps Ricky Hughes get into a coat at the donations and help center at First United Methodist Church in Phil Campbell. Ricky lost his home and Mary Williams and her family lost their homes. Yet Mary worked as a volunteer at the church helping others.

Kathy Whitfield of 164 Doris Road gets a hug from Marcie Kennedy of Madison while she cleans up her yard after the tornado.

Hands On Birmingham, a United Way agency, added more than 12,000 volunteers to its database within a week and a half of the tornado outbreak.

Their efforts included removing debris from the devastated communities of Concord and North Smithfield, working phone banks for the Emergency Management Agency and the American Red Cross, and unloading and distributing donations to storm survivors in Pratt City.

"There's a great network of people, nonprofits and churches all over town that are putting in tons of hours," Hands On Birmingham director Tree Gentle-Davidson said. "It's just a great thing to see: Alabamians helping Alabamians."

'Joy comes in the morning'
After sorting through the rubble and salvaging the remains, the toughest part came next.

Burying the dead.

Across the state, coroners began the agonizing task of trying to identify many of the 238 victims so their families could lay them to rest.

Identifying the bodies became a challenge, not only because of the sheer number of victims, but because of the circumstances surrounding their deaths.

Some were found in fields. Some didn't have any identification.

"Some of our victims were initially identified with tattoos," DeKalb County Deputy Coroner Bruce Wilson said. "Family members in other states would give verbal descriptions, then send family members to physically identify the person."

In St. Clair County, where 12 people were killed in the Shoal Creek Valley area, Usrey Funeral Home in Pell City handled services for nine of the victims.

"We've been so busy," funeral home director Steve Perry said. "We haven't seen tragedy on this type of scale."

About 350 mourners filled the pews and spilled out into the foyer of the funeral home to say their goodbyes to Ronnie Isbell, who was killed along with his daughter-in-law, Tammy Isbell, and granddaughter, Leah Isbell, when the tornado smacked the assisted-living center Isbell ran outside of Ashville.

Reflecting on a verse from Psalms 30, Pastor Lowell Douglas of Grays Chapel Baptist Church reassured the grieving that trouble does not always last.

"Weeping may endure for a night," he said, "but joy comes in the morning."

'That's how we are'
Gradually, life went on, although for many, it would never be the same.

In Hackleburg, the little town that the tornado threatened to wipe off the map, the community turned to the Hackleburg High Panthers baseball team for an escape and a sense of normalcy.

The EF5 tornado ravaged the elementary, middle and high school complex and destroyed most of the businesses around town, including the Piggly Wiggly and the Wrangler plant where many townspeople worked.

Above left: Concord Baptist Church was taking in food and clothing items all day the Saturday after the storm. Above right: Heavy equipment moves in quickly to load storm debris in Cullman.

The water tower, which proclaims Hackleburg as home of the 2007 state baseball champions, remained standing, though.

And so did the Panthers baseball team.

Five days after the tornado, the team was back on the field for a Class 1A playoff series against Cedar Bluff.

None of the players lost family members in the storm, but four lost their homes.

"You have to know Hackleburg to know we never considered canceling our season," junior Adam Sutherland said. "That's how we are.

"If one of us had died, we'd have played even harder for them."

Hackleburg defeated Cedar Bluff to advance to the state quarterfinals, where the Panthers were eventually eliminated by the South Lamar Stallions.

'We want to be back to normal'

The next step for those who lost their homes and their businesses was deciding whether to rebuild or relocate.

Thousands of tornado victims across Alabama faced that dilemma as they made choices that would reshape their communities.

Should they stay where they are rooted or make a fresh start elsewhere?

In Concord in west Jefferson County, 46-year-old Brady Houghton and his wife, Janeese, and their boys Lucas and Logan lost the three-bedroom, three-bath house that the Houghtons had just paid off in January.

"This one here," Houghton said, ruffling Logan's hair, "first thing he said was, 'Let's build back right here.' My wife? Not so much."

Janeese Houghton didn't want to live where she would have to face the daily reminders of the devastation, or listen to the constant clanging and banging of construction.

But they all wanted the same thing.

"We want to be back to normal as quick as possible," Brady Houghton said.

Cities, too, were faced with the daunting task of starting anew.

Tuscaloosa was still in the early stages of a massive cleanup when talk turned from recovery to rebuilding.

A week after the April 27 tornado, Mayor Walt Maddox established the Rebuild Tuscaloosa Task Force, and city leaders said they wanted to seize the opportunity to build a better Tuscaloosa.

"Not just better and stronger, but smarter," task force chairman John McConnell said.

"Even though it's a disaster, this is sort of a planner's dream — a means of making a change."

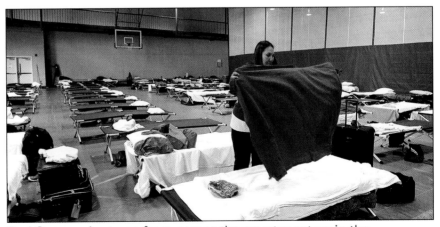

Red Cross volunteers from across the country set up in the Bashinsky Field House at Samford University. Melanie Fuentes of Salt Lake City makes her bed as she arrives.

119

April 27, 2011
Storm by storm

The National Weather Service confirmed more than 50 separate tornadoes on April 27, 2011, at the time this book went to press. That number could grow.

The following is a synopsis of each tornado. Details are from National Weather Service offices in Birmingham and Huntsville.

At least two waves of widespread, severe weather rolled over Alabama that day.

The first moved through during the early morning hours across north central Alabama and produced damaging straight-line winds and a few strong tornadoes.

The second wave spawned a number of supercell thunderstorms and long-lived, strong tornadoes across the northern two-thirds of central Alabama. Those tornadoes caused widespread and catastrophic damage across the state.

Following is the latest and best information on each storm.

Storms are listed based on the time they touched down, beginning with the earliest storms. A few tornadoes are listed at the end for which start times have not been established.

DANCY (PICKENS COUNTY)

EF-2 tornado; peak winds approximately 125 mph. Storm width: .8 mile. Distance: 21 miles.

Start time: 4:16 a.m. End time: 4:33 a.m.

No known injuries.

Began in Mississippi and entered Alabama in the vicinity of Tabor Road and Highway 17 in the Dancy community of Pickens County. The storm downed trees, damaged an outbuilding and an irrigation system.

NORTHERN REFORM (PICKENS COUNTY)

EF-2 tornado; peak winds approximately 120 mph. Storm width: 1,000 yards. Distance: 14 miles.

Start time: 4:30 a.m. End time: 4:42 a.m.

No known injuries.

Touched down near Phoenix Avenue, crossing Harris Road in a rural forested area, uprooting and snapping thousands of trees. The storm crossed Alabama 82 northwest of Reform where homes suffered minor roof damage and damaged trees. Crossing Alabama 17, the storm damaged several more homes and outbuildings.

HOLMAN TORNADO (PICKENS AND TUSCALOOSA COUNTIES)

EF-3 tornado; peak winds approximately 140 mph.

Storm damage width: 600 yards. Distance: 22.4 miles.

Start time: 4:41 a.m. End time: 5:02 a.m.

No known injuries.

Touched down south of Alabama 82 in far eastern Pickens County and uprooted many trees. The tornado crossed into Tuscaloosa County near the Holman community where the path grew to 400 yards, and the storm continued uprooting trees and tore the roof off a house, tossed a 3,500-pound trailer 100 yards and damaged homes, many by falling trees.

Three outbuildings or barns were damaged or destroyed. The tornado lifted 2.5 miles east northeast of Samantha.

BERRY (FAYETTE COUNTY)

EF-1 tornado; peak winds around 100 mph.

Width: 200 yards. Distance: 7.5 miles.

Start time: 5:07 a.m. End time: 5:15 a.m.

Four injuries.

Touched down along Alabama 18, four miles southwest of Berry where it damaged several barns and snapped and uprooted trees. Traveled into downtown Berry where several businesses and homes sustained wall and roof damage. The tornado lifted along Alabama 18 near Simmons Road.

COALING TORNADO (TUSCALOOSA/JEFFERSON COUNTIES)

EF-3 tornado; peak winds to 155 mph.

Damage width: 200 yards. Distance: 18.3 miles.

Start time: 5:17 a.m. End time: 5:35 a.m.

No known injuries.

Touched down southwest of Coaling off Staghorne Drive where trees were damaged. Storm paralleled Interstate 20/59 destroying some homes and damaging others. Continued northeast and damaged the Mercedes plant roof, blew down power poles and numerous trees. From there it continued through a rural area damaging trees before lifting in southwest Jefferson County at Old Tuscaloosa Highway and Lowetown Road.

PARRISH-CORDOVA TORNADO (WALKER COUNTY)

EF-3+ tornado; peak winds at least 140 mph.

Damage width: 300 yards. Distance: 19 miles.

Start time: 5:20 a.m. End time: 5:36 a.m.

No known injuries.

Began in rural southwestern Walker County east of Alabama 69 and south of Walker 6. Rapidly intensified and destroyed a home on Horseshoe Bend; tore through the Richardson subdivision and across Pleasantfield Road, destroying at least two mobile homes. The storm damaged or destroyed several homes, a mobile home and uprooted many trees in the Aldridge community. Moving into Cordova, downtown buildings suffered significant damage. The tornado crossed old U.S. 78 just east of the Mulberry Fork, snapping and uprooting trees before dissipating less than a mile north of U.S. 78.

ALTADENA TORNADO (SHELBY/JEFFERSON COUNTIES)

EF-2 tornado; peak winds up to 100 mph.

Damage width: 100 yards. Distance: 3.4 miles.

Start time: 5:50 a.m. End time: 5:54 a.m.

No known injuries.

Touched down west of the Valleydale Road and Caldwell Mill Road intersection. Moved north-northeastward across a residential area, snapping many trees that fell across power lines, automobiles, homes and apartments. Heaviest damage was along and just east of Caldwell Mill Road near the Cahaba River. The tornado lifted near Cahaba River Road.

CAHABA HEIGHTS TORNADO (JEFFERSON COUNTY)

EF-2 tornado; peak winds up to 120 mph.

Damage width: 200 yards. Distance: 7.9 miles.

Start time: 5:54 a.m. End time: 6 a.m.

No known injuries.

Touched down near Gresham School in the Mountain Brook/Vestavia Hills area and moved northeast across U.S. 280 in Cahaba Heights, eventually crossing Interstate 459 before lifting near Grants Mill Road east of the Liberty Park area. Hundreds of trees snapped and uprooted, many landing on homes causing significant damage. Most damage was in the Cahaba Heights area, west of the elementary school and north of U.S. 280.

ODENVILLE TORNADO (ST. CLAIR COUNTY)

EF-2 tornado; peak winds up to 120 mph.

Damage width: 200 yards. Distance: 3.9 miles.

Start time: 6:14 a.m. End time: 6:18 a.m.

No known injuries.

Touched down in a field southeast of the intersection of Alabama 174 and Isbell Road. Strengthening quickly, it struck two multi-story brick homes, significantly damaging both. The tornado continued northeastward before lifting near the intersection of Pleasant Valley Road and Cedar Road where a few trees were blown down.

JOHNSONS MILL TORNADO (CULLMAN/MARSHALL COUNTIES)

EF-1 tornado; winds up to 110 mph.

Damage width: 75 yards. Distance: 11 miles.

Start time: 6:20 a.m. End time: 6:40 a.m.

Touched down northeast of Cullman 1850, snapping numerous hardwood trees. As the tornado strengthened, it rolled a mobile home several times on Feemster Gap Road. Another mobile home to the northeast was blown several feet. The tornado moved through the Johnsons Mill community, damaging several barns. As it moved northeast, several chicken houses were destroyed. Damage continued along the peninsula between Big Springs Creek and Browns Creek on Guntersville Lake.

PLEASANT GROVE TORNADO (MARSHALL COUNTY)

EF-1 tornado; Winds up to 110 mph.

Damage width: 100 yards. Distance: 3.4 miles.

Start time: 6:30 a.m. End time: 6:40 a.m.

This first of three tornadoes south of Guntersville touched down near the intersection of Pleasant Hill Road and Section Line Road. The tornado moved northeast, crossing Pleasant Grove Road, uprooting hardwood trees and removing the steeple of Pleasant Hill Church. A wooden front porch of a nearby home was thrown about 100 feet.

LATTIWOOD TORNADO (MARSHALL COUNTY)

EF-1 tornado; Winds up to 110 mph.

Damage width: 50 yards. Distance: 5.7 miles.

Start time: 6:30 a.m. End time: 6:40 a.m.

The second of three tornadoes south of Guntersville touched down near Section Line Road and Beck Road in the Lattiwood Community. The tornado moved northeast, snapping numerous trees and power poles. Several barns were destroyed. The tornado lifted northeast of Wyeth Mountain Road.

ALBERTVILLE TORNADO (MARSHALL COUNTY)

EF-1 tornado; Winds up to 110 mph.

Damage width: 50 yards. Distance: 4.6 miles.

Start time: 6:30 a.m. End time: 6:40 a.m.

The third of three tornadoes just south of Guntersville touched down near the intersection of Highway 325 and Max Graben Circle southwest of Albertville. The tornado moved northeast, snapping numerous trees and damaging several homes. The tornado crossed U.S. 431 north of Albertville. A chicken house was destroyed on Arbor Acres Road.

GRANT MOUNTAIN TORNADO (MARSHALL COUNTY)

EF-1 tornado; Winds up to 90 mph.

Damage width: 50 yards. Distance: .3 miles.

Start time: 6:35 a.m. End time: 6:40 a.m.

This tornado briefly touched down on Crest Hill Road off Cathedral Caverns Highway on the south side of Grant Mountain. Trees were snapped and uprooted along the path, and a house sustained roof damage. The tornado lifted quickly.

PINE ISLAND TORNADO (MARSHALL COUNTY)

EF-1 tornado; Winds up to 105 mph.

Damage width: 50 yards. Distance: 1.6 miles.

Start time: 6:40 a.m. End time: 6:50 a.m.

The tornado touched down between Buck Island and Pine Island on Guntersville Lake. The tornado skipped northeast, snapping numerous trees along Alabama 79. The tornado touched down again on Pine Island and remained on the ground for several miles approaching the Jackson County line. Numerous homes sustained damage from falling trees. Additional surveys are needed to determine the full length and width of this path.

LAKE GUNTERSVILLE TORNADO (MARSHALL/DEKALB COUNTIES)

EF-2 tornado; Winds up to 120 mph.

Damage width: ½ mile. Distance 20 miles.

Start time: 7:10 a.m. End time: 7:18 a.m.

Initially touched down west of Guntersville Lake. The tornado continued northeast across Marshall 14 and across Cha-la-kee and Cotton Roads, where several homes had damage to shingles and numerous large trees were uprooted. The tornado moved northeast across Guntersville Lake and strengthened as it crossed Buck Island. Numerous trees were snapped and uprooted across the Buck Island community. Several power poles were snapped near their bases. Numerous homes in the Buck Island community had minor roof damage. Several piers and sheds were destroyed. The tornado crossed east over Guntersville Lake and struck Lake Guntersville State Park. Hundreds of trees were twisted, snapped and uprooted through the northern half of the state park. Several RV campers were damaged in the campgrounds. Minor roof damage was observed to the camp lodge. The tornado continued northeast, just to the east of Highway 227, were hundreds of trees were snapped and uprooted along the west-facing valley wall. The tornado moved northeast destroying a trailer and rolling another near Oliver Road, between Williams and Martin Drive. A barn and shed were demolished. The tornado crossed Highway 227 near Morgan Cove Road, twisting and uprooting several trees. The tornado weakened as it headed into

DeKalb County, with mainly large tree limbs snapped and twisted, and a few trees uprooted. The tornado appeared to dissipate between Grove Oak and Bucks Pocket State Park, near CR 19 and CR 544

ROSALIE TORNADO (JACKSON/DEKALB COUNTIES)

EF-2 tornado; Winds up to 120 mph.

Damage width: 200 yards. Distance: 6.6 miles.

Start time: 7:10 a.m. End time: 7:18 a.m.

The tornado began near Henagar, tracking northward, then lifted east of Rosalie. Numerous trees were snapped or uprooted from near Henagar northward. No less than three barns were heavily damaged. The tornado collapsed the west end of a home near Rosalie. Additional trees were snapped or uprooted before it lifted near the junction of Highway 71 and County Road 345.

ATHENS TORNADO (LIMESTONE COUNTY)

EF-0 tornado; Winds up to 85 mph.

Damage width: 150 yards. Distance: 6.7 miles.

Start time: 11:15 a.m. End time: 11:25 a.m.

Touched down near intersection of Limestone 24 and Batts Road, embedded in a larger region of straight-line wind damage. Numerous trees were down and witnesses indicated a funnel descended and lifted several times along the damage path. At Snake Road and County Road 24, numerous large trees were uprooted or snapped. Several homes had shingle damage. Dissipated after Browns Ferry Road.

DECATUR TORNADO (MORGAN/LIMESTONE COUNTIES)

EF-1 tornado; Winds up to 105 mph.

Damage width: 75 yards. Distance: 9 miles.

Start time: 11:20 a.m. End time: 11:30 a.m.

Touched down in a Decatur industrial park west of Red Hat Road. Damaged the roof of an industrial building and snapped several hardwood trees. This tornado continued east-northeast across the Tennessee River, snapping trees along Morgan 45 and Calhoun Community College. Pryor Field lost power at 11:28 a.m. as the circulation passed over the Limestone County airport. Dissipated before I-65.

TANNER TORNADO (LIMESTONE COUNTY)

EF-0 tornado; Winds up to 70 mph.

Damage width: 50 yards. Distance: 3.6 miles.

Start time: 11:23 a.m. End time: 11:28 a.m.

Formed in association with a secondary circulation that developed a few miles south of another tornado. Touched down near the intersection of Browns Ferry Road and Neely Road; uprooted trees and damaged signs near Tanner High School before dissipating.

CAPSHAW TORNADO (LIMESTONE/MADISON COUNTIES)

EF-1 tornado; Winds up to 110 mph.

Damage width: 200 yards. Distance: 24.2 miles.

Start time: 11:30 a.m. End time: 12:05 a.m.

Touched down south of Highway 72 in east Limestone County, uprooting trees. Moved northeast, snapping trees and removing shingles, crossing Capshaw Road near Old Railroad Bed Road. Numerous power poles snapped. Dissipated in the Deposit community.

MAGNOLIA SPRINGS TORNADO (LIMESTONE/ MADISON COUNTIES)

EF-1 tornado; Winds up to 110 mph.

Damage width: 100 yards. Distance: 3.2 miles.

Start time: 11:35 a.m. End time: 11:40 a.m.

Touched down west of Old Railroad Bed Road, producing roof and shingle damage. Moved across Magnolia Springs neighborhood. The most intense damage occurred east of Vine Cliff Drive, where numerous large trees were snapped at their base. Dissipated near Nichols Spring Branch.

WINCHESTER ROAD (MADISON COUNTY)

EF-1 tornado; Wind around 105 mph.

Width: 500 yards. Distance: 7.6 miles

Start time: 11:50 a.m. End time: 12:05 p.m.

Touched down near the intersection of Pulaski Pike and Cedar Point Drive. A concentrated area snapped hardwood trees and roof damage was observed near Green Meadow Road and again along the slope of Smithers Mountain in Mount Charron Estates and Valley View Estates neighborhoods. The tornado continued east with damage seen along Moore Mill Road north of Winchester Road. Dissipated near Briar Fork.

BUCKHORN HIGH SCHOOL TORNADO (MADISON COUNTY)

EF-0 Tornado; Wind around 85 mph.

Width: 100 yards. Distance: 3.4 miles

Start time: 11:55 a.m. End time: 12:05 p.m.

Touched down north of Rube Robinson Road. The path was embedded within a larger region of damage from straight-line winds. Many hardwood trees were snapped and sheared near Buckhorn High School. The tornado headed east-northeast across Winchester Road, shearing the tops of numerous trees before dissipating at Lewis Mountain.

HACKLEBURG TORNADO (MARION/ FRANKLIN/LAWRENCE/MORGAN/ LIMESTONE/MADISON COUNTIES)

EF-5 tornado; peak winds 210 mph.

Damage width: 1.25 mile. Distance 132.5 miles

Start time: 3:05 p.m. End time: 4:28 p.m.

Numerous injuries; at least 70 fatalities.

Appeared to touch down southwest of Hamilton near Highway 19 and County Road 22, damaging trees. The tornado quickly widened as it moved along Highway 43 southwest of Hackleburg. In Hackleburg it destroyed several subdivisions, Hackleburg High School and the Wrangler plant. At least 18 died there. From there it moved on to Phil Campbell, downing thousands of trees, destroying at least a hundred structures, leveling many homes and destroying hundreds of structures damaged. Vehicles were tossed 150 to 200 yards. At one point, a 25-foot section of pavement was sucked up and scattered. Multiple mobile homes destroyed, and mangled frames tossed 25 to 50 yards. The storm roard on through Oak Grove, into Lawrence County near the Mt. Hope area and on into Morgan County. Along the way, countless homes, restaurants, trees, chicken houses, power line towers, mobile homes and automobiles were destroyed. In Limestone County, the storm tracked near the Tanner community, still obliterating homes along a wide swath in both Tanner and Anderson Hills neighborhood in Madison County. More high tension power lines were damaged or destroyed. The tornado crossed into Madison County east of Limestone County prison, along Orvil Smith Road. Dozens of well-constructed homes were destroyed. The tornado tracked through residential areas along Bald Eagle Lane, Old Eli Road, and Ginnery Row. At least one fatality was confirmed here. The tornado lifted just south of Patterson Lane after twisting irrigation equipment and snapping additional trees. An EF-0 tornado with peak wind speeds of 70 mph redeveloped along Grimwood Road and Walker Lane south of Hazel Green, uprooting or snapping a few trees. The tornado weakened or may have lifted very briefly across northeast Madison County before strengthening again as it entered Franklin County Tennessee.

CORDOVA TORNADO(PICKENS/TUSCALOOSA/ FAYETTE/WALKER/CULLMAN/BLOUNT COUNTIES)

EF-4 tornado; peak winds around 170 mph.

Damage width: ¾ mile. Distance: 123 miles+

Start time: 3:38 p.m. End time: 5:50 p.m.

Dozens of injuries; 10 confirmed fatalities.

Touched down about three miles northeast of Pickensville and left a continuous path of damage to Cordova. East southeast of Berry along County Road 27/46 at Wilcut Road and southwest of County Road 83, mobile homes and trees suffered significant damage. The storm then crossed Corridor X and roared into the southwest side of Cordova, cutting a half-mile-wide swath of damage in downtown Cordova. The tornado then tracked to the northeast across Burton Chapel Loop Road and crossed the Mulberry Fork of the Black Warrior River. As the tornado crossed Mountainview Road, it increased from EF-03 to EF-4 strength, destroying a home and two mobile homes, tossing one at least 500 yards. At this site a bulldozer was flipped and a pickup truck thrown 200 yards. Other vehicles and trailers were also picked up by the storm and deposited up to a mile away. As the tornado neared old U.S. 78, it threw mobile homes at least 100 yards. Continuing toward the Sipsey community, the tornado destroyed more mobile homes, rising and falling in strength as it roared along. Many homes and mobile homes were destroyed or seriously damaged. The storm cut through a corner of Cullman County and then spun into Blount County where it passed near Sulpher Springs northeast of Bangor and into the town of Blountsville where it crossed U.S. 431 and damaged or destroyed many homes on Maple Drive. Continuing out of Blountsville, the storm destroyed and damaged more homes.

PANOLA (SUMTER/PICKENS COUNTY)

EF-3 Tornado; peak winds around 140 mph.

Width: .5 mile. Distance: 16 miles into Alabama from the Alabama/Mississippi state line.

Start time: 3:56 p.m. End time: 4:12 p.m.

No known injuries.

Moved into Sumter County from Kemper County, Mississippi, and crossed County Road 3, downing many trees. The tornado continued downing trees as it crossed Highway 17 at the intersection of County Road 34. As it continued through a pine forest, numerous trees were snapped at their base. No tree in the area was left standing. A large cinderblock building off County Road 85 had part of its roof blown off and an outer wall knocked down. The tornado began lifting at Alabama 14, north of the Sipsey River in southern Pickens County where there was minor tree damage.

SHOTTSVILLE TORNADO (MARION/FRANKLIN COUNTY)

EF-3 tornado; peak winds 150 to 160 mph.

Damage width: 3/4 mile. Distance: 19.1 miles.

Start time: 3:57 p.m. End time: 4:20 p.m.

Several injuries; at least six fatalities.

The tornado path began in Marion County near County Road 93 and Dry Creek Road. Several structures were damaged and many trees were snapped off and uprooted. The tornado continued northeastward and crossed U.S. 78/Corridor X west of Hamilton near the Bexar community. It strengthened to EF-3 strength as it crossed Highway 19 and County Road 20

where several homes were destroyed and at least six people lost their lives. The storm then moved across Highway 187 near the Franklin County line. Along the path, at least 25 homes, mobile homes and outbuildings were destroyed or damaged; at least five structures were obliterated. Hundreds of trees were downed. This tornado moved into south central Franklin County, where it continued for approximately 2 miles.

FLAT ROCK TORNADO (JACKSON/DEKALB COUNTIES)

EF-4 tornado; peak winds 190 mph.

Damage width: 1 mile. Distance: 28 miles.

Start time: 4:01 p.m. End time: 4:36 p.m.

Multiple injuries; at least 11 fatalities.

Began about three miles northeast of Section and rapidly grew to wind speeds of 150 to 170 mph and a path width of 1/2 to 3/4 mile as it roared northeast of Pisgah and north of Rosalie. Residents said the tornado was multi-vortex with as many as three tornadoes merging into one large tornado. Three were killed in three separate homes. Several vehicles were launched or swept several yards in different directions, in a few cases as much as 50 yards. Tornado winds grew up to 190 mph as it approached the Flat Rock and Higdon communities. The tornado killed another three at a residence southwest of Flat Rock. One well-built block foundation home exploded as the tornado struck, lifting and sweeping all its structure and contents downwind, in some cases several hundred yards. The tornado continued across the northern tip of DeKalb County in the Shiloh community. The tornado killed as many as 5 people in this area. Several cinder block foundation homes and mobile homes were destroyed. A senior citizen van was lifted and dropped in a field nearly 400 yards away. The tornado crossed into Dade County Georgia with a 1/4 to 1/2 mile wide path north of Highway 75.

TUSCALOOSA/BIRMINGHAM (GREENE/ TUSCALOOSA/JEFFERSON COUNTIES)

EF-4 tornado; winds up to 190 mph.

Damage width: 1.5 miles as it crossed Interstate 65. Distance: approximately 80.3 miles.

Start time: 4:43 p.m. End time: 6:14 p.m.

More than 1,000 injuries; at least 65 fatalities.

A supercell thunderstorm that began in Newton County, Mississippi, at 2:54 p.m. spawned this tornado. The supercell thunderstorm existed for seven hours and 24 minutes, traveling approximately 380 miles and producing several strong to violent tornadoes along the way. Thousands of businesses, homes, mobile homes and other structures were destroyed or severely damaged. Power systems failed. Countless trees and stretches of forest were destroyed. The tornado lifted just northeast of

Birmingham, but the thunderstorm continued on and produced other tornadoes along its path.

BRIDGEPORT (JACKSON COUNTY)

EF-4 tornado; winds up to 180 mph.

Damage width: 3/4 mile. Distance: approximately 20.5 miles.

Start time: 5:05 p.m. End time: 5:25 p.m.

Injuries unknown.

Touched down northeast of Fackler community, and damaged mobile homes. The tornado continued east-northeast and northeast of the Stevenson Airport twisted or flattened 24 high tension electrical truss towers. Near Jackson 255 and Jackson 256, the tornado reduced one home to its foundation. A compact car was thrown about 50 yards. To the northeast of the intersection two well-built homes were reduced to their foundations. This tornado continued northeast and destroyed a cinder block garage and damaged a mobile home along Sixth street southeast of Bridgeport. The tornado then crossed the Tennessee River and damaged trees as it crossed into Tennessee.

HALEYVILLE (MARION/WINSTON COUNTIES)

EF-3 tornado; winds 150 to 160 mph.

Damage width: 3/4 mile. Distance: 31.8 miles.

Start time: 5:10 p.m. End time: 5:51 p.m.

At least 10 injuries.

Touched down south of Hamilton near U.S. 278, County Road 2 and Philadelphia Road where trees were damaged. The tornado moved northeast and strengthened near the Pea Ridge and Whitehouse communities where several people were injured and several homes destroyed. The tornado moved into the Thornhill community and southern and eastern parts of Haleyville, producing significant damage. Winston Furniture Company and Fontaine Trailer Company suffered extensive damage. Many homes were destroyed or significantly damaged. Countless trees were snapped or uprooted as the storm moved through the forests of northern Winston County.

SAWYERVILLE/EOLINE TORNADO (GREENE/ HALE/BIBB COUNTIES)

EF-3 tornado; winds approximately 145 mph.

Damage width: 1 mile. Damage path length: 71.3 miles.

Start time: 5:30 p.m. End time: 6:55 p.m.

At least 50 injuries and seven fatalities.

Began near the Tombigbee River in southwest Greene County west of Tishabee on County Road 69 near Head Drive. It moved northeast across rural Greene County north of Forkland, destroying or damaging at least four mobile homes, two churches, three outbuildings and many trees. Two persons in Greene County were injured. Growing in strength, the storm crossed the Black Warrior River and moved into Hale County, passing through Sawyerville and then into the Talladega National Forest, but not before destroying or damaging numerous homes, mobile homes, a church and countless trees. At least 40 people were injured and six were killed in Hale County. The storm reached Bibb County through the national forest, moving northeast to Eoline before ending in Marvel. Several homes, mobile homes, one business, the Eoline Fire Station and countless trees were destroyed or damaged. Eight people were injured and one was killed in Bibb County. The storm ended near the Bibb/Shelby County line.

HUBBERTVILLE (FAYETTE COUNTY)

EF-3 tornado; winds 145 mph.

Damage width: .5 mile. Damage path length: 7.4 miles.

Start time: 6:06 p.m. End time: 6:14 p.m.

No known injuries.

Touched down 4.5 miles south of Bobo near Highway 43 where many trees were snapped or uprooted. The tornado moved northeast, leaving a wide swath of downed trees. The tornado crossed County Road 49, destroyed a home, several barns and outbuildings and damaged others. The tornado lifted near County Road 24, approximately two miles south of Bazemore.

ARGO/SHOAL CREEK/OHATCHEE/FORNEY TORNADO (JEFFERSON/ST. CLAIR/CALHOUN/ETOWAH/CHEROKEE COUNTIES)

EF-4 tornado; winds up to 180 mph.

Damage width: Up to 1.25 miles. Damage path length: 72 miles in Alabama. Storm continued into Georgia.

Begin time: 6:23 p.m. End time (at Georgia state line): 7:47 p.m.

Numerous injuries; several fatalities.

Touched down near Argo between Deerfoot Parkway and Advent Road, north of Interstate 59; then moved east across the interstate into St. Clair County. It tracked near Margaret and north of Odenville, then strengthened and widened considerably. Moving along County Road 22 through Shoal Creek, the tornado caused extensive damage. Several homes were destroyed or heavily damaged. The storm then crossed Neely Henry Lake into Calhoun County, damaging a number of homes and mobile homes on the lake's eastern shore, north of Ohatchee. Several homes were obliterated. At this point the storm had reached its widest point of 1.25 miles with winds near 180 mph. Roaring through northern Calhoun County, south of Etowah County, the storm destroyed a number of homes and mobile homes. A small church on Rocky Hollow Road near the Webster Chapel community was leveled. The storm moved into the edge of Etowah County, southeast

of Reaves, clipped a small portion of Calhoun County one last time then moved into Cherokee County where it damaged many more homes and mobile homes. The tornado appeared to weaken briefly as it moved through Frog Mountain, but then it widened and strengthened once again before reaching County Road 45 north of Rock Run on County Road 29 south of Forney where it leveled a home. The tornado then moved into Georgia at County Road 28. Along its path, hundreds of structures were destroyed and damaged and many thousands of trees were uprooted or snapped.

WATEROAK TORNADO (HALE/BIBB COUNTIES)

EF-1 tornado; winds around 105 mph.

Damage width: 150 yards. Damage path length: 5.5 miles.

Begin time: 6:50 p.m. End time: 6:59 p.m.

No known injuries.

Touched down two miles southwest of Wateroak in Hale County and moved northeast into the Talladega National Forest, ending in southwest Bibb County, two miles southwest of Mertz. A mobile home and a business were torn up along with numerous trees. The storm ended in southwest Bibb County.

MARVEL (BIBB/SHELBY COUNTIES)

EF-1 tornado; wind around 105 mph.

Damage width: 50 yards. Damage path length: 5.4 miles.

Begin time: 7:32 p.m. End time: 7:38 p.m.

No known injuries.

Touched down in a forested area of northeast Bibb County west of the intersection of Bibb 65 and 10. It traveled northeast, snapping off dozens of pine trees. The tornado lifted in a grassy field north of Shelby 10 between Blossom Street and Springbrook Lane.

PINHOOK/FAUNSDALE (SUMTER/MARENGO/PERRY COUNTIES)

EF-2 tornado; winds of 120 mph.

Damage width: 350 yards. Damage path length in Alabama: 32.34 miles.

Begin time: 7:46 p.m. End time: 8:40 p.m.

Three known injuries.

Formed in Mississippi and had a total destruction path of 123 miles before lifting in Alabama. Moved into west central Alabama from Clarke County, Mississippi, the storm came across southeast Sumter County, central and northeast Marengo County and extreme southwest Perry County. It uprooted trees south of Sumter 42 and Lock 3 Road. The storm passed north of Linden near Pin Hook and north of Chickasaw State Park along U.S. 43, and then northeast through the Faunsdale area where it destroyed and damaged several homes and

injured as least three people along Nash Road south of Faunsdale. Continuing northeast, the storm passed north of Uniontown, crossing Highways 61 and 183. It damaged buildings and uprooted trees in that area. The tornado dissipated east of Highway 183 in southwest Perry County.

PELL CITY TORNADO (ST. CLAIR/TALLADEGA COUNTY)

EF-0 tornado; winds of 80 mph.

Damage width: 50 yards. Damage path length: 2.3 miles.

Begin time: 7:55 p.m. End time: 7:50 p.m.

No known injuries.

This brief tornado touched down east of Pell City about 100 yards south of Interstate 20 at Exit 162. It moved across the interstate and then lifted along U.S. 78. Several trees were blown down and snapped off.

LAKE MARTIN TORNADO (ELMORE/TALLAPOOSA/CHAMBERS COUNTIES)

EF-4 tornado; winds up to 170 mph.

Damage width: 1/2 mile. Damage path length: 44.1 miles.

Begin time: 8:12 p.m. End time: 9:09 p.m.

Several injuries and nine fatalities.

Touched down along County Road 209 near Meadowview Drive where it snapped a few trees. From there the tornado quickly intensified as it moved northeast through Dexter, widening and damaging several homes. It continued strengthening as it moved through a mobile home park at the intersection of Middle Road and Auction Barn Road, destroying 10 mobile homes and killing four people. The tornado continued east to the Mount Hebron Road area, destroying several homes, businesses, two churches and an agricultural nursery. It then crossed Lake Martin just south of the Highway 63 bridge, significantly damaging to many homes in the Wyndermere area. At this point the tornado had expanded to approximately 1/4 mile wide. It then moved into Tallapoosa County south of County Road 34 and grew to a half mile wide and strengthened more. Damage was widespread and several multi-story homes were demolished. The tornado crossed Highway 49 north of Jones Road where it destroyed two homes and rolled a pickup truck for 120 yards. It crossed U.S. 280 east of Dadeville, causing significant damage to a number of home and business structures in its path. The tornado then crossed into western Chambers County, passing north of Sikes along County Road 54 north of Sikes where one home was destroyed. The tornado weakened as it moved northeast across County Road 66 and ended north of County Road 51.

VINCENT-LOGAN MARTIN TORNADO (SHELBY AND TALLADEGA COUNTIES)

EF-1 tornado; winds of 105 mph.

Damage width: 200 yards. Damage path length: 6.8 miles.

Begin time: 8:15 p.m. End time: 8:24 p.m.

No known injuries.

Touched down south of the town of Vincent on Shelby 62, uprooting dozens of trees. The tornado traveled to the northeast, dropping trees along its path. Continuing northeastward, the tornado damaged the east end of Logan Martin Dam and continued through a couple of residential neighborhoods, snapping and uprooting trees. Fallen trees damaged one house on Shaw Lane alongside Logan Martin Lake.

MARION (PERRY COUNTY)

EF-1 tornado; winds of 90 mph.

Damage width: 200 yards. Damage path length: 4.39 miles.

Begin time: 8:48 p.m. End time: 8:53 p.m.

No known injuries.

Touched down about one mile west of Highway 35 along Perry 38 and damaged trees in a 50-yard-wide area. The storm crossed Highway 45 and skirted Faith Chapel Baptist Church, snapping and uprooting several nearby trees. The tornado dissipated as it moved east of Perry 4.

WHITE PLAINS (CHAMBERS COUNTY)

EF-1 tornado; winds up to 110 mph.

Damage width: 150 yards. Damage path length: 5.3 miles.

Begin time: 9:19 p.m. End time: 9:28 p.m.

No known injuries.

Touched down along Chambers 225, uprooting and snapping several trees and doing significant roof damage to one home. The tornado moved east-northeast, crossing Chambers 178 and Chambers 176 where many more trees were uprooted and snapped. From there the tornado tracked east-northeast before lifting near Chambers 267 where additional trees were snapped and uprooted.

FINLEY CREEK (CHAMBERS COUNTY)

EF-1 tornado; winds up to 90 mph.

Damage width: 100 yards. Damage path length: 5 miles.

Begin time: 9:29 p.m. End time: 9:38 p.m.

No known injuries.

Touched down along Chambers 267 north of the ending path of the White Plains tornado. The paths did not join and both damage widths were relatively small. Damage at Chambers 267 included several sheared and uprooted trees. Continuing northeast, the tornado crossed Chambers 270 where more trees were snapped and an outbuilding suffered minor roof damage. The tornado lifted along Chambers 278 where there was minor tree damage.

VERBENA (CHILTON COUNTY)

EF-0 tornado; winds of 80 mph.

Damage width: 50 yards. Damage path: 1.9 miles.

Begin time: 9:48 p.m. End time: 9:50 p.m.

No known injuries.

Touched down at the intersection of U.S. 31 and Chilton 24, northeast of Verbena, where it uprooted a few oak trees. The tornado continued northeast and crossed the intersection of Chilton 59 and Chilton 24, damaging the metal carport of one home, the roof of a mobile home and several trees. The tornado quickly dissipated east of Chilton 59.

CULLMAN (CULLMAN/MORGAN/MARSHALL COUNTIES)

EF-4 tornado; winds of 190 mph.

Damage width: 1/2 mile. Damage path: 47 miles.

Begin time: 2:43 p.m. End time unknown.

Injuries unknown.

Near Grandview, significant structural damage occurred to several residences. The tornado continued to track northeast toward Cullman where some of the worst damage occurred northeast of U.S. 31 and 278. Several small retail buildings were destroyed along with near destruction of a large church. The tornado continued its track northeast crossing Highway 157 then creating additional damage north of Highway 69 between Simcoe and Pleasant View. North of Fairview along CR 1559 and CR 1564, two homes were destroyed. Further northeast along CR 1589, major structural damage occurred to several old (early 1900s) homes and numerous trees were debarked. The tornado crossed out of Cullman County briefly into extreme southeast Morgan County near the town of Hulaco. Significant damage occurred between Hyatt Bottom Road and Blocker Road, east of Highway 67. Several cinder block and old construction homes were destroyed and numerous trees were snapped and sheared toward the base. In northwest Marshall County worst of the damage occurred from the Morgan/Marshall county line, along Hog Jaw Road, northeast to U.S. 231 (about 3 miles north of Arab). Along Hog Jaw Road, a large storage shed with farm equipment was destroyed with some large machinery tossed 10 to 20 yards around the shed. Mount Oak and Frontier Roads were hardest hit where a cinder block/cement home was nearly wiped clean. Debris from this home was thrown 50-100 yards. Along Frontier Road, a large brick home was nearly wiped from its foundation with

several large trees ripped out of the ground and missing. Further northeast along the path, along Walnut Ridge, a one-story home was severely damaged and a trailer was tossed into a tree. Several concrete power poles were bent over as the tornado crossed U.S. 231. The tornado continued toward Union Grove. Several homes had significant damage where the top stories and roofs were destroyed along with some external walls collapsed. The tornado weakened as it crossed the Tennessee River.

RAINSVILLE (DEKALB COUNTY)

EF-4 tornado; winds of 175 mph.

Damage width: 3/4 mile. Damage path: 33 miles.

Begin and end times not established.

Multiple injuries and deaths.

Path begins in the Lakeview community northeast of Geraldine, then tracked northeast through Fyffe, Rainsville, and Sylvania and eventually into northern DeKalb County south of the Cartersville community. Extensive damage occurred in the Rainsville and Sylvania communities where houses were removed from foundations, trees were debarked and a few mobile homes were destroyed. Along DeKalb 27 southeast of the border with the Sylvania community, several homes were destroyed with partial block and mortar foundations remaining. Some hardwood trees were stripped. Farther northeast along County Road 112 just east of Sylvania and near the High Point community, a couple of electrical transmission metal truss towers were bent and twisted. South of the Ider community, several homes were destroyed with exterior and interior walls blown away. South of Cartersville and near the Blevins Mill community, trees were snapped and felled, but the damage path was reduced to about 50 yards as the tornado appeared to weaken.

HANCEVILLE (CULLMAN COUNTY)

EF-2 tornado; winds of 120 mph.

Damage width: 1/2 mile. Damage path: 26 miles.

Begin and end times not established.

Injuries unknown.

Touched down east of Cold Springs, toppling and snapping numerous trees. The tornado tracked northeast, snapped trees and damaging chicken coops. After crossing Interstate 65 south of Dodge City, the tornado strengthened as it approached Wallace State College in Hanceville. Eight large metal power poles were bent over above the base and several campus buildings had metal roofing torn off. A mid-rise under construction had its windows blown out, while the high-rise building sustained minor damage. To the south of the main track, in Hanceville proper, many large trees were toppled onto houses. East of Hanceville the tornado continued toward Walter and then to south of Holly Pond.

RHODESVILLE TORNADO (LAUDERDALE COUNTY)

EF-1 tornado; winds of 90 mph.

Damage width: 100 yards. Damage path: 1.8 miles.

The begin and end time of this early-morning tornado has not been established.

Injuries unknown.

Touched down north of the Smithsonia community. A storage shed was demolished and a second partially damaged. The tornado lifted before touching down again at the corner of County Road 189 and County Road 62. The front of a church was shifted four inches and metal trusses in the roof were twisted.

WATERLOO TORNADO (LAUDERDALE COUNTY)

EF-1 tornado; winds of 110 mph.

Damage width: 200 yards. Damage path: 9 miles.

Begin and end times not established.

Injuries unknown.

Touched down one mile north-northeast of the Waterloo community. Numerous trees snapped and two docks along Second Creek were damaged. Southeast of the intersection of County Road 90 and County Road 21, three homes were damaged. This tornado continued to produce significant damage as it progressed to the northeast. The tornado then tracked into a wooded area and moved into Tennessee.

MADISON TORNADO (LIMESTONE/MADISON COUNTIES)

EF-1 tornado; winds of 90 mph.

Damage width: 50 yards. Damage path: 11.8 miles.

Begin and end time not yet established.

Injuries unknown.

Began near I-65 between mile markers 342 and 343. The tornado tracked northeast, producing minor, sporadic damage. It traveled through rural Limestone County and through the city of Madison, where it uprooted several trees and damaged several homes. The most notable damage occurred along Balch Road near Kentucky Drive and where Wall Triana meets Gooch Lane. The tornado lifted near Nance Road.

Fatalities

238 TORNADO DEATHS
Number of deaths in each county from April 27th tornadoes.

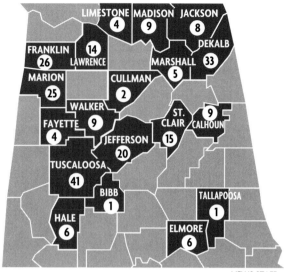

NEWS STAFF

Bibb County

Brent
Ricky Paul Smith, 55

Calhoun County

Ohatchee
Ruby Douthitt, 61
Tina Forrest, 49
Michael Forrest, 54
Francis Arvella Jones, 72
James Romaine, 65

Piedmont
Angel Stillwell, 13

Webster's Chapel
Vernon Spencer Motes, 33

Wellington
Linda Sue Lipscomb, 63
William Lipscomb, 67

Cullman County

Cullman
Lloyd Winford Harris, 68

Johnson Crossing
Keenan Jonathan Sullivan, 20

DeKalb County

Exact location unknown
Chelsie Black
Charlotte Bludsworth, 36
Belinda Boatner
Gene Bullock, 65
Marcella Bullock, 64
Jewell Ewing
Emma Ferguson, 6
Jeremy Ferguson, 34
Tawnya Ferguson, 32
Hannah Goins, 3
Kenneth Graham, 56
Linda Graham, 61
Ruth Hairston, 90
Harold Harcrow, 74
Patricia Harcrow, 75
Jody Huizenga, 28
Lethel Izell, 86
Jimmy Michael Kilgore, 48
Courtney McGaha, 15
William Michaels, 70
Martha Michaels, 72
Eulah Miller
Ida Ott
Timothy Ott
Ester Rosson, 81
Peggy Sparks
Terry Tinker
Daniel Vermillion, 42
Jidal Vermillion, 44
Herbert Wooten, 70
Juanita Wooten, 70

Ider
Judith White, killed in a fire
  caused by the storm
Wayne White, killed in a fire
  caused by the storm

Elmore County

Eclectic
Candice Hope Abernathy, 23
Kammie Abernathy, 5
Melissa Ann "Missy" Myers
  Gantt, 43
Alice Herren Lee, 74
Martha Ann Gray Myers, 67
Rebecca Herren Woodall, 70

Fayette County

Berry
Jeffery Kemp, 60
Reba Kemp, 60
Leon Spruell
Sylvia Spruell

Franklin County

East Franklin
Donald Ray Heaps, 48
Kelli Thorn Morgan, 24
Michael Morgan, 32

Phil Campbell
Nila Black, 68
Zan Reese Black, 45
Jeffrey Dewight Cotham, 35
Jack Cox, 78
Charlene Crochet, 41
Donnie Gentry, 63
Patricia Ann Gentry, 50
Lester William Hood, 81
James Robert Keller Jr., 67
Rickey Ethan Knox, 10
Amy LeClere, 33
Jay W. LeClere, 45
Dagmar Leyden, 56
Edna Lucille Bradley Nix, 89

Martha Lou Pace, 64
Claudia I. Mojica, 38
Edgar Mojica, 9
Georgia Schribner, 83
Jack E. Tenhaeff, 67
Sonya Black Trapp, 47
Carroll Dean "C.D." Waller, 76
Gerri Waller, 64

Double Springs
Donna Renee Berry, 52

Hale County

Greensboro
Cora L. Brown, 68
Gerald C. Brown, 70

Sawyerville
Jerry Lee Hodge, 64
Henry Lewis, 26
Frankie Lunsford, 55
Elizabeth C. White, 25

Jackson County

Pisgah
Kathy Gray Haney, 46
Herbert Satterfield, 90
Ann Satterfield, 81

Higdon
Janie Shannon, 80

Flat Rock
Shelby Jean Shannon, 58
Elease Whited, 75
John Whited, 77

Bridgeport
Branen Warren, 13

Jefferson County

Pleasant Grove
Iva Mae Cantrell, 73
James Jerry Clements, 66
Cheryl Denise Cooper, 47
Canatha Hyde Earley, 71
Reba Jones, 75
Carrie Grier Lowe, 26
Ramona Sanders-Walker, 47
Louella Bell Thompson, 81
Tracy A. Traweek, 39
Nancy L. Wilson, 56

Concord
Janet Dickinson Hall, 55
Jennifer Leonard Jones, 26
Haley Alexis Kreider, 8
Michael David Kreider, 10
Michelle Pearson Kreider, 30
Ernest C. "Ernie" Mundi Jr., 53

Cahaba Heights
Milton Edward Baker Sr., 68

Pratt City
Bessie Brewster, 72

Forestdale
Kenneth Ray Nation, 64

McDonald Chapel
Deniece Presley, 57

Lawrence County

Chaleybeate
Aurelia Guzman, 12
Donald "Duck" Ray, 73
Edward Vuknic, 66

Hillsboro
Zora Lee Jones Hale, 80

Langtown
Lyndon Lee "Doby" Mayes, 74
Mary Mayes, 76

Mt. Moriah
Allen Oneal Terry, 49
Herman Oneal Terry, 80

Moulton
Mike Daworld Dunn, 58

Mount Hope
Matthew Chase Adams, 21
Earl Lewis Crosby Sr., 63
J.W. Parker, 78
Horace Grady Smith, 83
Helen Smith, 84

Limestone County

Tanner
Carol Jan McElyea, 67
Janice Dorothy Peden Riddle, 54
Roger Glen Riddle, 55

East Limestone
Shannon Gail Sampson, 39

Madison County

Harvest
Katie Cornwell, 15
Harold Fitzgerald, 65
Milinia Nicole "Nikki" Hammonds, 32
Ronnie McGaha, 40
Bobby Joe Moore, 61
Frederick Post, 72
Rachel Renee Tabor, 37

Toney
Gregory John Braden, 59
Philomena Muotoe, 79

Marion County

Hackleburg
Rodney Gene Ables
Bridget Barnwell Brisbois, 34
Robbie Cox, 68
Tina Donais
Chris Dunn
Charles Tommy Garner, 75
Mae Garner, 79
Ed Hall, 53
Teresa Gay Hall, 50
Kaarlo Jokela, 76
Donna Lee "Leah" Jokela, 77
Linda Faye Knight, 57
Freddie Lollie, 81
Vickey Lollie, 55
John Lynch
Cledis Inez McCarley
Vicki Lynn McKee, 47
Faye O'Kelley
Ken Vaughn, 24

Hamilton
Michelle Brown, 43
Tammy Johnson, 52
Jacob Ralph Ray, 5
Virginia Revis, 53
Allan Mark Wideman, 49
Jeanette Cochran Wideman, 52

Marshall County

Ruth
Ann Hallmark, 54
Phillip Hallmark, 56
Shane Hallmark, 37
Jennifer Hallmark, 31
Jayden Hallmark, 17 months

St. Clair County
Oberia Layton Ashley, 86
Ronnie Isbell, 56
Tammy Isbell, 31
Leah Isbell, 7
Bertha S. Kage, 91
Thomas Carl Lee, 64
Stella "Mae" Lovell, 97
Sandra Pledger, 68
Albert Sanders, 44
Angie Sanders, 43
Charlie Andrew Wolfe, 68
Nettie Ruth Wolfe, 68

Pell City
Precious Necale Fegans-Hartley, 27

Moody
Sandra Gayle McCrory, 56

Tallapoosa County

Dadeville
Katherine Massa, 70

Tuscaloosa County

Tuscaloosa
Minnie Acklin, 73
Jerry Artis, 51
Scott Atterton, 23
Jennifer V. Bayode, 35
Caiden Blair, 2 months
Michael Bowers, 3
Loryn Brown, 21
Mary Bryant, 43
Graham Davie, 55
Ta' Christianna Dixon, 11 months
Danielle Downs, 24
Makayla Edwards, 5
Melgium Farley, 58
Cedria Harris, 8
Keshun Harris, 5
Ashley Harrison, 22
Shena Hutchins, 26
Carolyn Ann Jackson, 50
Jacqueline Jefferson, 45
Thelma Krallman, 89
Davis Lynn Latham, 57
Tennie Mozelle Lancaster, 95
Velma T. Leroy, 64
Dorothy Lewis, 61
Thomas D. Lewis, 66
Yvonne Mayes, 61
Christian A. McNeil, 15 months
Zy'Queria McShan, 2
Melanie Nicole Mixon
Perry Blake Peek, 24
Lola Pitts, 85
Terrilyn Plump, 37
Kevin Rice, 36

Annie Lois Humphries Sayer, 88
Judy Sherrill, 62
Morgan Marlene Sigler, 23
Marcus Smith, 22
William Chance Stevens, 22
Justin Leeric Thomas, 15
Patricia Turner, 55
Willie Lee Turner III, 21

Walker County

Argo
Wesley Starr, 45
Lucille Waters, 89

Cordova
Jonathan Doss, 12
Justin Doss, 10
Annette Singleton, 46
Jackson Van Horn, 24

Oakman
Kathleen Brown, 64

Sipsey
Pam Jett, 43
Harold "Junior" Jett, 47

128